Models for Teaching Writing-craft Target Skills

Other Maupin House books by Marcia S. Freeman:
Building a Writing Community: A Practical Guide
Crafting Comparison Papers
Listen to This: Developing an Ear for Expository
Teaching the Youngest Writers: A Practical Guide

Other Maupin House books by Susan Koehler:
Crafting Expository Papers
Purposeful Writing Assessment: Using Multiple-Choice Practice to Inform Writing Instruction

Models for Teaching Writing-craft Target Skills

Revised and Updated Second Edition

Marcia S. Freeman and Susan Koehler

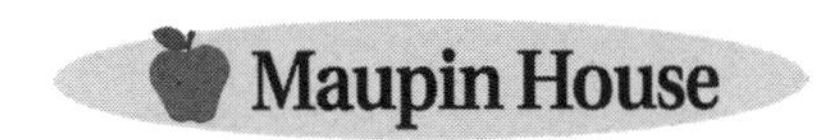

Models for Teaching Writing-craft Target Skills
Revised and Updated Second Edition
By Marcia S. Freeman and Susan Koehler

Cover design: Studio Montage
Book design: Marble Sharp Studios
Editor: Kendall M. Sharp

Library of Congress Cataloging-in-Publication Data

Freeman, Marcia S. (Marcia Sheehan), 1937-
Models for teaching writing-craft target skills / Marcia S. Freeman and Susan Koehler. -- Rev. and updated 2nd ed.
p. cm.
Includes bibliographical references.
ISBN-13: 978-1-934338-81-0 (pbk.)
ISBN-10: 1-934338-81-8 (pbk.)
1. English language--Composition and exercises--Study and teaching. 2. Children--Books and reading. 3. Children's literature--Bibliography. I. Koehler, Susan, 1963- II. Title.
LB1576.M7294 2010
372.62'3--dc22
2010033902

ISBN-13: 978-1-934338-81-0

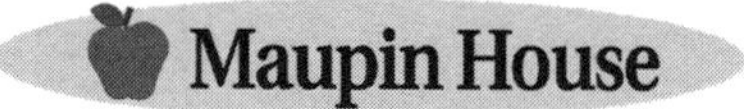

Maupin House Publishing, Inc.
2416 NW 71st Place
Gainesville, FL 32653
www.maupinhouse.com
800-524-0634
352-373-5588
352-373-5546 (fax)
info@maupinhouse.com

10 9 8 7 6 5 4 3 2

Dedication

My work in this book is dedicated to my wonderful husband, John Koehler, and our five beautiful children: Dylan, Tyler, Emily, Shelby, and Hillary. We've shared so many books together, and have so many yet to share.

—S.K.

Table of Contents

Acknowledgements

This book would not have been possible without the help of a number of dedicated educators. I am especially grateful to Luana K. Mitten and Rachel Chappell, whose comments and counsel during the planning and drafting of the manuscript, as well as their input into the bibliographies, was invaluable.

I also want to thank the many teachers and librarians from schools implementing CraftPlus®, who contributed lists of their favorite books and identified the writing craft the authors used.

Marcia S. Freeman

The updated edition of this book is the product of the foresight and efficiency of the great folks at Maupin House Publishing, Inc. They listen to and seek to meet the needs of teachers everywhere. Their support for authors and educators is to be applauded.

Also deserving of gratitude is Jennifer Bonell, who worked tirelessly to design and create the matrices. She found titles that would make quality literature models accessible to teachers of both English and Spanish-speaking students. Her efforts have expanded the diversity of this resource so that it may reach a greater number of teachers and students.

Of course, the original version of this book was written by Marcia S. Freeman, a champion of best practices in the teaching of writing. Her foundation of Target Skills® for teaching writing craft has revolutionized writing instruction in countless classrooms. It is impossible to estimate the number of teachers and students she has affected, but I am grateful to be among them.

Susan Koehler

Introduction

Teaching with Literature Models

Writing craft is the wonderful set of skills and techniques that writers know and use to make their writing clear and interesting. Therefore, craft instruction is a critical component of effective writing education. That instruction, provided in a classroom writing-workshop environment, is the key to writing competency. The writing workshop provides the setting and conditions for students to learn and practice writing craft and use the writing process—prewriting, composing, getting a response, revising, and editing. Writing-craft lessons provide the tools students need to effectively organize, compose, and revise.

In *The Rise and Fall of English*, Robert Scholes, the Andrew W. Mellon Professor of Humanities at Brown University, advises, "*Our range, our capabilities go no further than craft. Even in creative writing courses, craft is all that can be taught.*" He also tells us, "*Our aim should be to help students learn how to produce a good, workmanlike job with a written piece whenever they need to. It means mastering the medium through the study of models.*"

If you teach writing, you have probably already recognized the value and validity of Professor Scholes's observation and are centering your writing instruction on craft. A vital part of your instruction is showing students how other authors have applied the craft skills you are teaching. This book provides the tools to make that task easily accessible for teachers.

How to Use This Book

This book begins by building a foundation of sound, craft-based practices for teaching writing. In the first chapter, you will learn manageable, effective strategies and instructional routines for introducing craft to the writing workshop environment. You will learn to differentiate instruction to meet the needs of individual learners, and you will understand how picture prompts, guided and interactive writing activities, and literature models can become powerful catalysts for well-crafted writing.

The second chapter is dedicated to genres. We will explore the power of literature models from various genres in facilitating the integration of writing and content-area instruction. You will delve into the specific characteristics of various forms of expository writing and see how non-fiction literature models can be used to support learning across disciplines.

In the third chapter, you will be immersed in specific writing-craft skills, called Target Skills®. This chapter is a convenient resource for understanding and demonstrating specific elements of craft. It is essentially a glossary of craft elements, complete with definitions, discussions, and examples. Along with each craft skill, corresponding literature models are conveniently listed for ready access.

The final chapter of this book is guaranteed to become a well-worn resource in the writing classroom. This is where you will find four matrices listing the literature models for writing-craft skills that span models of writing. The matrices are alphabetized by title, and the Target Skills are listed in alphabetical order as well.

The fiction literature-model matrix identifies models for thirty-two writing-craft Target Skills. The models include many popular picture books and intermediate texts. The non-fiction literature-model matrix provides a listing of many non-fiction texts that can be used to model twenty-three Target Skills.

The third matrix lists poems that can be used to demonstrate twenty-two different craft skills. Poems are brief and easy to display, but are often overlooked as literature models. The poems listed are easy to locate in popular anthologies and Internet searches.

The final matrix is a listing of Spanish literature models to support teachers of bilingual education. While Spanish-speaking students are working to master the English language, the skills and concepts introduced to other students through English-language models can be taught, modeled, and applied in Spanish.

Why Revisit *Models for Teaching Writing-craft Target Skills?*

The first edition of this book was published in 2005. Since that time, the idea of teaching craft and the reliance on using literature models have both exploded in popularity. Wonderful new titles have emerged in children's literature, and technology has become a common tool for managing classroom tasks. This second edition of Marcia S. Freeman's original text expands the instructional framework of writing craft and provides updated lists of literature models with a cross-reference to the respective Target Skills contained in each.

So what's new in this book?

In this updated version, a matrix is dedicated to poetry literature models. Poetry is brief and concise, providing an opportunity to display and analyze an entire piece together and making the identification of craft elements obvious.

Another addition is the inclusion of Spanish language models. Bilingual education is a vital part of modern American schools. If we are to provide all students with a solid foundation in authentic craft instruction, we need to give them the tools by which to learn. Spanish-language models will meet the needs of a growing number of bilingual students.

The rest of the matrices have been expanded to include a greater number of texts that are easily accessible and common to classrooms. A wealth of award-winning titles and well-written non-fiction pieces will help you, the teacher, access the tools needed for authentic, literature-based writing instruction.

You'll find an array of intermediate literature models included in this second edition, and they are indicated with asterisks in the matrices. The intermediate models selected contain multiple examples of the craft skills referenced, making it easy for the teacher to skim the book and locate pertinent passages.

Exploring Literature

What hasn't changed? The idea that writing craft Target Skills can be found in multiple genres, including non-fiction books, is carried over from the original text and expanded within these pages. Students are required to write for multiple purposes and across various genres. The vast collection of different types of literature—from non-fiction to poetry—enables you to demonstrate skills in genre-specific context.

In the years since the original version was published, the term "mentor text" has become a part of standard pedagogical vocabulary. However, in this book, we will continue to use the term "literature model." The focus on high-quality literature must not be compromised. We don't want to lose that emphasis. Children must understand that in your classroom environment, students are **authors** and the reading material you share to model writing craft is **literature**.

Chapter One

Teaching Craft

"Artistry does not come from the quantity of red and yellow paint or from the amount of clay or marble but from the organizing vision that shapes the use of these materials. It comes from a sense of priority and design."
—Lucy Calkins, *The Art of Teaching Writing*

What Is Craft?

Well-crafted pieces are lively and engaging. Sentences vary in length and style. The writing leads readers to visualize characters, settings, actions, and events. Word choice is precise, descriptions are vivid, and literary devices are used to guide the reader in making inferences. Thesis statements and arguments are well-supported and convincing. If a piece is well-crafted, the reader inadvertently drifts into the world created by the author.

Children may not be able to identify the specific elements of writing craft employed by a favorite author; however, they certainly know when literature is lively and engaging. They want to read these works over and over again, enjoying the magic of a clever tale and the beauty of skillfully woven language. When we expose children to high-quality literature, they understand the power of the written word.

The elements of craft that work together to create such writing are no mystery. You can name them, model them, and teach your students to employ the same craft skills used by their favorite authors. Marcia Freeman calls them Target Skills. This book will guide you in teaching your students to transform their writing with Target Skills and will give you a resource for locating specific literature models so that you will have examples of well-written author's craft at your fingertips.

Writing Craft and the Reading Connection

Reading researcher T. Shanahan (1997) notes that "Awareness of an author's choices is central to effective critical reading, but this information is well hidden in text, and children become aware of it rather late in their development. Writing, because it affords one an insider's view of this aspect of text, provides a powerful, complementary way of thinking about reading that would not be available if reading and writing were identical."

Students can learn to recognize the choices authors make if they are making these very same ones themselves. A major area of author choice is writing craft. When we begin teaching craft skills in kindergarten, children do not have to wait until "rather late in their development" to become aware of these choices.

When students, in their independent reading, are able to recognize the craft authors have chosen, you can be assured that they have internalized that craft. As you equip students with the concepts and terminology of writing craft, they will enthusiastically share their recognition of Target Skills applied by their favorite authors.

You can take it as an equally good sign when students tell you about the lack of craft in the books they are reading. Not all published books are good models of writing craft, and students trained to look for craft love to point out ones that are not. They make suggestions for revisions that could make the writing more lively and engaging.

Teaching Writing Craft

In some craft lessons, your goal will be simple awareness and recognition of the craft skill. In others, your goal will be students' application or attempted application in writing. The choice will be determined by your young writers' current experiences and fluency levels.

In a well-constructed, school-wide writing program, young writers get to see the same writing-craft skills modeled with increasing sophistication as they progress through the grades. Even with ample practice, it can take several months or even years for them to learn to use a skill fluently and gracefully.

Children increase their knowledge of writing craft by seeing the skills they are studying used in printed text. Continually encouraged by us, they will learn to write by copying the pros. Let's examine the process for teaching a writing-craft lesson using a literature model.

INTRODUCE THE TARGET SKILL:

1. **Name the Target Skill, define it, and present a literature model:**

   "Because readers need to visualize, writers must create imagery, and one way to do that is with **strong verbs**. Strong verbs are action verbs that are specific and easy to picture. Let's listen to this selection: The squirrel SCURRIED up the pine tree. What was the strong verb in that sentence?" Students may respond, "Oooh, SCURRIED!"

2. **Discuss the technique:**

   "Can you visualize what is happening if you are not looking at a picture? Which is more helpful? The squirrel WENT up the pine tree, or the squirrel SCURRIED up the pine tree?"

3. **Model the technique orally, using and talking about a photo. Model two or three sentences:**

   "In my photo, a horse is NIBBLING an apple." Invite your students to respond to the verb nibbling with a thumbs-up and an "Oooh, NIBBLING!" Continue with two more sentences about the horse and what it is doing. "The horse's mane is HANGING down his neck." Thumbs-up. "Oooh, HANGING!"

TRY IT OUT ORALLY:

4. **Students, in partnerships or in a circle with you, try the technique out orally.**

   They each talk about a photograph they have previously selected. Photographs are an excellent aid in writing instruction. When students select pictures that match their background experience, they will have plenty to say. They will share the content vocabulary—words pertinent to the subject of the picture—with other students. Guide them through the articulation of sentences that feature a person, animal, or object engaged in action. Continue the thumbs-up and "Oooh" responses for strong verbs.

TRY IT OUT IN WRITING:

5. **Students try the technique out on their own:**

   They write a few sentences about their photo. The level of students' verb choices depends on their vocabularies, which in turn depends on prior vocabulary training, reading, and life experiences. But regardless of the level, each student can hit the target.

Note: About 80 percent of the writing students do in writing workshop should be pure practice. Think of learning to write as analogous to learning a musical instrument. Practice sessions consist of working on skills, then working through a piece in which those skills are applied. Practice pieces are not evaluated; they are guided and encouraged. After ample practice, a developed piece is taken through the entire writing process (from pre-writing to editing) and presented for evaluation.

SHARE:

6. **Peers respond to student writing:**

   Students say or read their sentences to another student. The listener compliments the writer's use of the Target Skill with a sticker or a color mark.

AFTER INSTRUCTION AND INTERACTIVE PRACTICE:

7. **Students practice the Target Skill:**

   They practice using Target Skills in their independent writing, such as in literacy centers, science journals, literature response pieces, and in personal journals. Practicing writing-craft skills in different venues encourages students to take risks and play with writing craft. It is through this kind of practice that students become creative and competent writers.

ASSESSMENT:

8. **Students apply the Target Skills in an assessed piece:**

   Once students have had ample opportunity to practice a Target Skill or skills, you will want to see if they can apply the skills to a prompted piece. You may choose to use a photo, verbal, or written prompt. They might take the piece through the entire writing process (pre-write, compose, peer conference, revise, and edit) or write a rough draft in a timed session.

   The rubric criterion for this assessed piece is the application of one or more of the specific, pre-identified Target Skills. Note how this gives every student an opportunity to succeed and adds objectivity to the holistic scoring process.

Using Literature Models

As you use literature models when teaching writing-craft skills, you should bear in mind the following principles:

- Books have two elements: **content** and **craft**. Always read a book to students for its content before analyzing it for the writing craft the author demonstrates. During your initial reading, children will want to, and should, focus on content. During a subsequent reading session, in which you invite open discussion of the book as you and your students explore it, draw their attention to the writing craft you intend to teach next.
- Always read literature that is well-written (employs rich vocabulary and active verbs; is organized, engaging, imaginative, accurate, pleasant-sounding, and well-illustrated). Look for literature that is filled with the writing craft identified in this book.
- Look for writing craft in all the books and magazines you regularly use throughout your instructional days. The learning potential for children from familiar text is great. Age-appropriate non-fiction pieces will show children that craft skills can be applied across various genres.
- Use literature from assorted genres to develop your students' ears for the different genres. For instance, students who hear a lot of informational text learn that its authors usually proceed from the general to the specific. The writer explains what a whale looks like before he gets into the details about how it breathes.
- In intermediate grades and higher, use children's picture books freely. These students will appreciate the format, and because they can easily understand its content, they are able to concentrate on its writing craft.
- ELL/ESOL students and students with learning difficulties also benefit from the use of children's picture books. Identifying and discussing writing craft in high-interest texts (regardless of reading level) supports their own practice of writing craft and provides experience with figurative language.
- When using intermediate texts, skim books in advance to locate and mark the examples of craft skills you wish to model. Ask students to identify examples of craft in their own reading. You will be surprised how rich your library of models will grow when you have children identify Target Skills in their reading.
- Keep literature models accessible to children and refer to them frequently when discussing the skill. "Remember how Tomie dePaola used descriptive attributes in *Strega Nona*?" Referencing the models will reinforce the students' identification of and familiarity with the modeled skill.

Note: Writing craft is the same for writers of all ages. For example, writers from six to ninety-six need to use strong verbs to help their readers visualize. Age-related differences show up in the sophistication level of the skill application, which reflects the level of the writer's vocabulary and life experiences.

Models from the Classroom

Be sure to create your own "teacher models" when you are introducing a new skill. Plan your teacher models in advance, but act as though you are generating them on the spot. Your students will be automatically engaged because they are watching these models come to life. Remember to think out loud as you create your model. You will demonstrate not only the craft skill, but also a thought process your students can emulate.

Writing teacher Dan Holt reminds us, "Sure, you could and should show polished professional examples to your students, but it makes all the difference when your students see you doing the same activity you have asked them to perform. And frankly, they need to see the activity performed to the degree of proficiency that they can realistically hope to achieve."

Teacher models are personal and accessible. While well-written published models are critical to effective writing instruction, teacher models are dynamic. They are happening right before the eyes of your students. Literature models demonstrate a skill; teacher models demonstrate a process.

Once students have some familiarity with the skill and process, use interactive models to form a bridge from published authors and teacher examples to independent student application. Begin with an idea, and ask students to contribute ways the skill can take shape within the context of your idea. Work with students to think, discuss, write, and revise a brief application of the skill. Interactive models allow students to actively participate and feel a sense of ownership over the model created.

As students begin to employ Target Skills in their writing, you can select exemplary student models to demonstrate the application of a craft skill. These models are authentic and usually apply the skill in a way that is within the reach of their peers. Students need to see how other young writers apply the craft and say to themselves, "I can do that, too!"

After your instruction, when students are working to apply the Target Skill being taught, circulate and pre-select exemplary student models to share with the class. After your workshop time, asking students to share these models is a great way to showcase pieces that "hit the target" and reinforce the skill for the rest of the class.

You can save student models by copying or scanning them, so that you can use them to review skills at a later time, or to demonstrate the application of the Target Skill in subsequent years. After a few years, you will have quite a storehouse of student models! Children enjoy seeing the work of other children and you'll be amazed at how motivating student models can be.

Student model of onomatopoeia as a beginning technique:

__Crash!!! Boom!!! Smash!!!__ Bob was working.
—Hillary, first grade

Student model of strong verbs:

*I slowly **climbed** out of bed this morning. I **scrubbed** the teeth in my mouth so hard they were white as snow. Then I **brushed** the rat's nest on my head until it was as straight as a ruler and **pulled** it into a ponytail.*
—Darbi, fifth grade

General Writing Skills and Genre-associated Skills

Many writing craft skills can be applied across genres. These general writing skills can be grouped together as **descriptive skills**. They include strong verbs, descriptive attributes, specificity, and other elements of craft that make writing lively and engaging. These skills help readers form visual images and connect to the text.

Descriptive skills should be taught and reviewed throughout the year. Students should practice applying them in multiple genres, and they should be modeled in multiple genres as well. Integrate descriptive skills into content-area studies. For instance, scientific observations can be enhanced by the use of descriptive attributes. Physical education can put strong verbs into concrete action. Specificity can be a vehicle for teaching capitalization of proper nouns.

While descriptive skills are applied across genres, some skills are more often associated with specific genres. For example, narrative pieces rely heavily on time (*After sunset; Later that day*) and place (*At school; When we reached the park*) transitions. Narrative skills are abundant in children's literature, and narratives are what we usually read aloud to children or what they choose to read independently.

Students are frequently asked to write expository pieces. Therefore, we need to find and use non-fiction models that provide examples of the format and skill set associated with expository writing. Expository writing often includes time and place transitions, but also uses additive (*Another reason; Additionally*), frequency (*Sometimes; Occasionally*) and progression (*First of all; Next; Finally*) transitions.

Additive, frequency, and progression transitions are more often found in brief articles than in trade books. For this reason, they are not included in the matrices in the fourth chapter of this book. You can find models of these types of transitional devices in more succinct pieces, like articles in non-fiction magazines for young people. An excellent resource is *Listen to This: Developing an Ear for Expository* (Freeman, M., Maupin House, 1997). This unique book contains a collection of expository articles that demonstrate the skillful use of multiple Target Skills.

Be creative in looking for models of different types of expository text. Recipes, directions for crafts, games, and experiments can make great procedural models. Editorials and opinion pieces in newspapers and children's magazines can serve as models of persuasive and opinion writing. Non-fiction texts and informational articles in substantive periodicals are ripe with genre-specific expository skills. These models are usually brimming with descriptive skills as well!

Genre-associated skills help define different styles and formats of writing. Point these skills out and model them in genre-specific pieces. Teach students to apply them where they are most functional—whether to advance a narrative or to signal a change in content. Learning to use genre-associated skills appropriately is a sign of mature writing.

A matrix devoted specifically to non-fiction models is included in the final chapter of this book. Be sure to add your own titles to this matrix as you find models in your collection of periodicals and non-fiction texts.

Use genre-specific literature models during your direct instruction, and also use them during individual and small group workshop activities to build awareness of Target Skills. Have students search through genre-specific literature models, creating lists of examples of a Target Skill. After writing a genre-specific piece, have them search their own writing to create a similar list.

See the following examples:

A list of time and place transitions in *The Mud Pony: A Traditional Skidi Pawnee Tale* retold by Caron Lee Cohen:

And every nightfall
As he slept
At daybreak
At the third nightfall
Every day
Finally
For three days
He ran to his corral
Just before daybreak
One day
So at last
Then
Then one night
There was once
When the boy got back to camp
When the boy left the big tepee
When the boy woke up at daybreak
Years passed

A student's list of time and place transitions from her own narrative:

As we got in the car	*Two months after that*
Forty-five minutes earlier	*We went to the water park*
One hour later	*When we got home*

—Mary, fifth grade

A list of progression transitions in a procedural piece, "Illustrating a Book is Kind of Like This" by Frank Remkiewicz, as printed and analyzed in *Listen to This*, by Marcia S. Freeman:

So, the first thing I do is	*Next*	*When I am happy*
Then I go into	*Then I finish*	*It takes a couple of months*
When I am finished	*Soon*	

A student's list of progression transitions in her procedural piece:

First	*After that*	*Finally*
Next	*Then*	

—Erin, fifth grade

Organizational schemes vary among genres as well. Narratives are told in chronological order; therefore, planning schemes should be developed in a linear pattern. Procedural writing is presented chronologically and also requires linear planning. However, all other forms of expository writing—comparison, informational, persuasive—are organized by grouping related details. These pieces should be developed by listing and sorting details.

The mental processes we must go through to organize our expository writing are what we commonly refer to as **critical thinking skills**. These skills are prominent objectives in the scope and sequence of every education-improvement plan. Writing instruction is an excellent vehicle for achieving these objectives.

Every expository writer discovers that writing **is** thinking—we can't write coherently about a topic we haven't thought about and organized. At the same time, the very act of writing helps us develop our thoughts and refine our organization.

Sorting and classifying, comparing, creating analogies, similes and metaphors, seeing patterns, sequences, and other logical relationships between objects, people, events, and ideas—these are all critical thinking skills. They are also critical organizing and composing skills for writers.

Thus, good writing instruction teaches young students critical thinking skills and how to apply them to communicate effectively. Whether students do any writing after they leave school or not, they need these skills to succeed in their jobs and in their lives. Be sure to give them opportunities to write for various purposes, multiple audiences, and across every area of the curriculum.

Picture-prompted Writing

Much of the writing students are required to do is prompted. We generally think of prompts as being written statements to which students respond. However, prompts can come in the form of pictures. A picture-prompted writing model is a handy way to introduce a Target Skill at any grade level.

For your model, you can use the cover of a Big Book, a poster, or a digital photograph projected on a screen. Display the picture to the whole group and use it to write a teacher model or an interactive piece. The process you will model consists of selecting a picture, talking about it, and writing about it.

When having students respond to picture prompts, you will need a large collection of colorful pictures.

Ask parents, friends, neighbors, and relatives to gather color pictures for your class. Magazines like *National Geographic* and *Ranger Rick* are a wonderful source, and you can often find them at garage sales or used bookstores. Laminate the pictures you collect or place them in plastic covers.

A photograph is a concrete aid—children can hold it, feel it, and talk about it. Show them how to choose pictures that match their personal experiences and interests. This will ensure that their writing will be authentic and that they'll have plenty to say about the picture. Photographs help students who might be inclined to say, "I don't know what to write about."

Your collection should include children engaged in play, work, sports, eating, etc.; insects, birds, reptiles, mammals, fish, etc.; rural and urban scenes; and so on. Encourage children to select a picture about something they know, something they can do, or a place where they might have been. Remind them of the Target Skill they will put into their writing.

Arrange students in pairs or small groups and have them talk about the pictures before they write. Circulate around the room and encourage students to apply the Target Skill orally. When the students have finished conferencing (five minutes is usually sufficient), use the sharing technique of asking young writers to compliment their partners: "Which of you heard your partners hit the target? Please tell us your partners' names and what they said was happening." Listen to several children's examples. Sharing in this fashion is critical for the development of your classroom writing community.

After discussion and response, students will be ready to write about their pictures, applying the Target Skill in a descriptive piece. Frequent use of picture prompts will familiarize students with these procedures and facilitate the kind of writing that leads to active visualization for readers.

Note: Professional photo cards you can use as individual picture prompts are available from Maupin House Publishing, Inc.

Categories of Target Skills

You may be familiar with CraftPlus®, a comprehensive K-8 writing curriculum built upon the work of Marcia Freeman and published by Maupin House Publishing, Inc. With CraftPlus, teachers learn to deliver Target Skill instruction in a workshop environment. Target Skills are identified for each grade level in the *CraftPlus Daily Writing Lessons*, a teacher's guide to writing instruction across the scope of an entire school year.

CraftPlus categorizes Target Skills into three distinct groups: **organizational skills**, **composing skills**, and **conventions**. Organizational skills are those skills needed to structure a piece of writing, including pre-writing, planning, beginnings, ending, and other skills that provide form and sequence.

Composing skills are those skills that engage the reader, make the author's meaning clear, and add aesthetic quality to a piece of writing. Composing skills include strong verbs, descriptive skills, literary devices, and various types of supporting details. Conventions, of course, cover language mechanics like punctuation, capitalization, spelling, and grammar.

When clustering skills together in a unit of study, Freeman suggests pulling skills from each of these categories to ensure well-rounded writing development. CraftPlus organizes skills within genre blocks—groups of skills that work together within a particular genre. In each genre block, organizational skills, composing skills, and conventions are taught and practiced in isolation and then are applied together within a genre piece.

Throughout instruction, literature models are used to provide examples of Target Skills as they are artfully applied by well-known authors. You can build your own genre block by selecting a set of skills that work together within a genre—teaching, modeling, and practicing the skills in isolation, and then having students apply the skills in an assessed genre piece.

The following is a sample genre block for four weeks of instruction in a descriptive writing:

WEEK ONE:

Composing Skill: Strong verbs

Literature Model: *The Wind Blew*, by Pat Hutchins

Monday and Tuesday: Introduce the skill, identify the skill in the literature model, have students practice applying the skill in pairs or small groups, and then have students practice applying the skill individually using various action-oriented picture prompts. Share exemplary student models.

Organizational Skill: Listing

Literature Model: Read list poems from *Falling Down the Page: A Book of List Poems*, Georgia Heard, ed.

Wednesday and Thursday: Discuss and model lists, have students work together to make lists inspired by the poems (things in your classroom, around your school, sounds they hear, foods they like, etc.), and then have students work individually to develop lists. Ask all students to share items from their lists.

Friday: Mini-assessment of strong verbs and lists. Have each student select an action-oriented picture prompt and make two lists, a list of things and a list of actions (strong verbs) in the picture. Students should use their lists to create a list poem modeled after one of the poems read as a model.

WEEK TWO:

Composing Skill: Descriptive attributes

Literature Models: *When I Was Young in the Mountains*, by Cynthia Rylant and *The Important Book* by Margaret Wise Brown.

Monday and Tuesday: Introduce the skill, identify the skill in the literature models, have students practice applying the skill interactively with you, and then in pairs or small groups. Next, have students practice applying the skill individually using various scenic picture prompts, listing colors, shapes, sizes, and other visual characteristics. Share exemplary student models.

Convention: Commas in a series

Wednesday and Thursday: Continue reviewing descriptive attributes, pointing out the use of commas in a series in the literature models. If students have mastered visual attributes, encourage the use of sensory attributes like taste, smell, and texture. Students should write complete sentences, including lists of descriptive attributes separated by commas.

Friday: Mini-assessment of descriptive attributes and commas in a series. Have each student select a scenic picture prompt and write one or two descriptive sentences that include lists of descriptive attributes separated by commas.

WEEK THREE:

Organizational Skill: Beginning technique: onomatopoeia

Literature Models: *Berlioz the Bear*, by Jan Brett and *Pancakes, Pancakes!* by Eric Carle

Monday and Tuesday: Discuss onomatopoeia and how it can be used to hook the reader at the beginning of a piece. Identify the skill in the literature models, have students work with you to list examples of onomatopoeia, and then have them write possible introductions to the mini-assessments they've written during the past two weeks. Share exemplary student models.

Organizational Skill: Ending technique: universal word

Literature Models: *Off We Go!* By Jane Yolen and *Sylvester and the Magic Pebble* by William Steig

Wednesday and Thursday: Introduce universal word endings and discuss how they can bring conclusion to a piece. Identify the skill in the literature models, have students work with you to list examples of onomatopoeia, and then have them write possible introductions to the mini-assessments they've written over the past two weeks. Share exemplary student models.

Friday: Mini-assessment of onomatopoeia beginnings and universal word endings. Have students select a picture prompt and write an onomatopoeia beginning and universal word ending.

WEEK FOUR:

Genre Piece: Apply all skills in a descriptive piece that is taken through the entire writing process, from pre-writing and planning to revising and editing.

As you approach a new school year, determine the Target Skills your students should master, as well as any skills you wish to teach at an awareness level. Select genres appropriate for the age level of your students and sort the Target Skills among the genres. Gather your literature models and be prepared to show students how "the pros" apply these Target Skills. Be sure to review descriptive skills in a spiraling manner, as they are foundational to every genre.

When you explicitly teach and practice the skills in isolation, and then apply multiple skills in a genre-specific piece, you are first giving your students the tools needed for success, and then you are giving them a purpose for writing. Using literature models to provide exemplary use of the skills you are teaching will help students build concepts and set goals that are within their reach. You will find that these essential ingredients form a powerful instructional cycle.

Assessment

While we have established the importance of ample practice in the development of writing skills, assessment is a necessary step in determining mastery, monitoring progress, and planning for subsequent instruction.

Assessment must reflect instruction, so use a scoring device that identifies the Target Skills that were taught and practiced. Holistic rubrics are popular but can be so general they lack objectivity. When using a rubric, it is best to create one that identifies your specific instructional objectives, or Target Skills.

The CraftPlus writing curriculum includes multiple-skill rubrics after each genre block. These rubrics help create objectivity in holistic scoring and can identify areas of strength and opportunities for growth. Take a look at this multiple-skill rubric for the descriptive genre block included on the previous pages:

Target Skills	**3** **Student applies skills competently and creatively**	**2** **Student applies skill competently**	**1** **Student attempts to apply skill**	**0** **Student does not attempt to apply skill**
Strong verbs				
Descriptive attributes				
Listing				
Beginning technique: onomatopoeia				
Ending technique: universal word				
Commas in a series				
Final Score: ______________________				
Teacher Comments: ______________________				

Create multiple-skill rubrics to use for scoring complete pieces. Tell students which skills you will be evaluating up front. Allow them to self-assess and make improvements before turning in an assessment piece. You will find that providing a list of objectives will give your students guidance in the revision and editing process.

If you are assessing only one Target Skill, you can use a single-skill rubric. The descriptors for each score point remain the same, but you will evaluate only the application of one Target Skill. Single-skill rubrics are useful for mini-assessments.

Assessing students' complete pieces with multiple-skill rubrics also proves to be a helpful progress-monitoring tool. You can use these rubrics to pinpoint specific individual strengths and identify opportunities for growth. With small groups and individuals, you can re-teach writing-craft Target Skills that have not been mastered, or take accomplished students up to the next step of complexity in applying Target Skills. Assessment, used in this manner, is a potent vehicle for differentiation and mastery of skills.

If you are assessing students' abilities to apply Target Skills in their writing, you will need to assign a written piece. However, if you want to find out if students understand the concepts and terminology you have introduced, multiple-choice assessments can be quick and easy indicators of mastery.

Purposeful Writing Assessment (Koehler, S., Maupin House, 2008) is a resource filled with quick multiple-choice assessments of the concepts and terminology you will be teaching when you introduce Target Skills. This resource, also available from Maupin House, provides pre- and post-tests for organizational skills, composing skills, and conventions. Strategies for re-teaching and remediation accompany each test.

Make the most of your instructional time by planning ahead, modeling throughout, allowing ample time for practice, and evaluating student progress on a regular basis. Check your students' understanding of terminology and concepts and their application of skills taught. As you identify opportunities for growth, apply re-teaching and remediation strategies as needed to individuals, small groups, or the entire class.

Tools of the Trade

Understanding the discipline of writing, its various genres, and the writing craft that lures and captivates readers are just the foundational elements that shape an effective writing instructor. Students also need to understand your expectations in a very tangible way.

Modeling is an instructional strategy integral to many quality lessons across the content areas, especially when new skills are being introduced. We demonstrate the process of working through an equation in math; we provide examples of science fair experiments before launching students into creating their own; we show them how to place their feet, bend their knees, and position their weight in a batting stance. **Modeling is a part of teaching**.

As writing instructors, we model by integrating high-quality literature models into our practice. In the next chapter, we'll explore various genres of literature and discuss the intricacies of each. Survey your classroom collection to see if each genre is well represented. We want to be sure to wrap our students in a print-rich environment that is as diverse and highly engaging as we want their writing to be.

Chapter Two

Learning through Literature

"Whether inscribed on rock, carved in cuneiform, painted in hieroglyphics, or written with the aid of the alphabet, the instinct to write down everything from mundane commercial transactions to routine daily occurrences to the most transcendent ideas—and then to have others read them, as well as to read what others have written—is not simply a way of transferring information from one person to another, one generation to the next. It is a process of learning and hence, of education."
—Vartan Gregorian

Best Practices in the Teaching of Writing

Writing instruction has evolved from a by-product of reading—its focus being proper letter formation and flawless mechanics—to a self-contained discipline with a well-defined process and complex array of sub-skills. In modern practice, schools tend toward discipline-isolated and skills-based approaches in all areas of the curriculum. Unfortunate side effects of this structure are either the tendency for writing to be squeezed out of the curriculum due to time constraints, or the fractured disconnect between writing and reading instruction.

In 2010, researchers Steve Graham and Michael Hebert, along with the Carnegie Corporation of New York, published *Writing to Read: Evidence for How Writing Can Improve Reading*. Their research findings support the idea that reading and writing complement each other to the extent that reading skills are improved by literature-based writing instruction. In other words, teaching students to think like writers can aid them in unraveling layers of explicit and implicit meanings in texts. The report offers three suggestions for teachers:

1. Have students write about the texts they read.
2. Teach students the skills and processes that go into creating text.
3. Increase how much students write.

Each of these suggestions begins with literature. A classroom rich in literature will nurture the growth of young readers and writers. This finding is not new. The inverse relationship and complementary interconnectedness of reading and writing have been firmly established by Donald Graves, Lucy Calkins, and Timothy Shanahan, to name only a few.

In 2004, the National Council of Teachers of English (NCTE) published a position statement on the teaching of writing that emphatically proclaims the connection between these two language processes. Among their instructional implications, NCTE notes:

> *"Overall, frequent conversations about the connections between what we read and what we write are helpful. These connections will sometimes be about the structure and craft of the writing itself, and sometimes about thematic and content connections."*

The use of high-quality literature models as a vehicle for teaching writing craft opens the door for frequent, substantive dialogue about literature and a view of literary works from the author's perspective. Through this dialogue, we can connect reading and writing with meaning and purpose.

As you begin to consider the genres you will cover over the course of a school year and the Target Skills you will teach within each genre, begin assembling your literature models. Read with a writer's eye. As you find exemplary models, tab pages, set books aside, and make lists for future reference. Prepare for your conversations about structure and craft.

In this chapter, we will explore the use of literature—both fiction and non-fiction—to teach students about genres and literary formats. You will gain an awareness of some models and strategies for using them. Of course, given the complementary relationship of reading and writing, your use of literature models will not only benefit your students' writing, but the development of writing craft will also increase their facility with literature.

Literature Models

The term **literature model** has been supplanted in modern educational jargon by the term **mentor text**. Both terms represents the same concept—skillfully written pieces that demonstrate the artful application of writing craft. The use of one or the other is simply a matter of style and choice.

In this book, we have chosen to use the term **literature models**. Although it may seem dated, the focus of the language is literature, and this focus should not be understated. Writers are artists who choose words with purpose and precision. Their words build images, convey meaning, and flow with an intended rhythm.

In many cases, the craft comes quite naturally to writers. Authors do not generally review their work counting the similes, checking onomatopoeia off the skills list, or creating a metaphor simply to prove they can do it. The writing is not contrived; it is formed with integrity and carries an authentic aesthetic quality. The skills are a natural undercurrent, largely unnoticed until identified.

When these same skills are new for your students, they will tend to over-generalize them, over-use them, and construct pieces that sound somewhat contrived. This is part of the learning process. With continued practice, they will grow and develop the ability to internalize the craft and focus on the message. This is the point at which they have developed a mature command of language.

The bridge that will carry them from fledgling writers to mature young authors is exposure to artfully constructed examples of craft. Be sure to choose authentic, high-quality literature models and make them a foundational piece of your writing instruction.

There are a few different types of literature models you will find in this book. Many of the models are picture books. These books are generally brief, engaging, and abundant with craft. Use picture books freely with older students. Your focus is not the theme or the reading level of the text; your focus is the craft, and these books provide rich examples of writing craft.

While you can use picture books as models with students of all ages, there are also benefits to using intermediate texts with older students. Generally, the vocabulary will be more mature and the example may be developed with more fullness and depth. Quite possibly, these models are books your students are reading or books that are part of your language arts curriculum.

The drawback to intermediate models is that the Target Skills are more difficult to locate in the sea of text. When you find examples of craft in extended texts, use sticky notes or tabs to mark pages. Encourage your students to identify Target Skills in their individual reading and your storehouse of models will grow exponentially.

Poetry is a genre often overlooked as a source of models for writing craft. This book contains a matrix listing poems that can be used to model Target Skills. Use a variety of genres when modeling writing craft. Your students will benefit from the range of text structures—they will learn to read and comprehend across an array of styles and genres as well as learning the intricacies of effective writing.

Non-fiction books are rapidly growing in popularity with students. They can also play a major role in your writing instruction. The majority of writing your students will be required to complete in school and in life will most likely be non-fiction. You will need well-crafted non-fiction models in your collection. This book dedicates one matrix to non-fiction titles. Use these books to model Target Skills and to integrate writing with your content-area instruction in a meaningful way.

Using Non-fiction Text

Students are required to produce non-fiction text in many situations. They write and present informational reports, conduct and explain research, perform and explain science experiments, and take notes to summarize important concepts.

In your print-rich classroom, be sure to have an assortment of non-fiction texts. As discussed earlier, these texts come in the form of books or informational magazines. Because you will use non-fiction texts as literature models, look for writing that is lively and engaging. For example, one way that authors engage readers in non-fiction text is through the use of pronouns to address the reader.

Compare these texts and notice how pronouns that address the reader create engaging text:

ENGAGING THE READER	NOT ENGAGING THE READER
Wetlands:	
If you visit a wetland, wear your boots.	Wetlands are very muddy places.
Wetlands provide food for birds. Food for us.	Wetlands provide food for birds and for people.
When we turn on our faucets, out comes clean, fresh drinking water.	When a faucet is turned on, out comes clean, fresh drinking water.
The Human Body:	
Your body has many parts and they all work together.	The human body has many parts and they all together.
Your bones change and grow with the rest of you.	Bones change and grow with the rest of the body.
Your heart is a muscle that pumps blood into every part of your body.	The heart is a muscle that pumps blood into every part of the body.
Kids for the Earth:	
We also use water for drinking and cleaning.	Water is also used for drinking and cleaning.
We use trees to make paper and to build houses.	Trees are used to make paper and to build houses.
It's our earth. Let's all keep it clean and beautiful.	It's everyone's earth. It should be kept clean and beautiful.

As you read non-fiction text, point out devices used by authors to engage readers. Reread well-written sentences and reserve non-fiction models to revisit when teaching additional writing-craft skills. When examining the craft in non-fiction text, make lists of engaging phrases and text structures. Maintain these lists in your classroom and keep them in an accessible location so they can serve as resources for students as they write.

SAMPLE PHRASES THAT ENGAGE READERS IN NON-FICTION TEXT		
Pronouns	*Imperative Statements*	*Questions*
If you look...	Examine...	Can you imagine...?
I think...	Listen...	Could it be...?
I wonder...	Look closely...	Did you ever wonder...?
We can...	Picture...	Have you ever...?
You can see...	Watch...	What do you think?

The organization of non-fiction text is important to point out to students. Understanding organizational structures will aid them in their writing and in their comprehension of non-fiction text. Chronological order guides story writers, but expository writers must find other logical and natural ways to present information or explain things. They must help their readers deal with many facts and ideas, make sense of them, and remember them. Here are some organizing techniques they employ:

- Moving from general to specific
- Using natural divisions within a topic
- Following a logical order, based on place or time
- Presenting a sequence of steps in a process
- Using alphabetical order
- Comparing two people, places, or things
- Ordering a series of arguments by importance or impact

Help students analyze non-fiction texts to determine their organizational structures. This process aids in comprehension and employs the thought path students will need to follow when they organize their own non-fiction pieces.

Use graphic organizers to dissect non-fiction pieces. Have students identify main ideas and supporting details, paragraphing strategies, and beginning and ending techniques. Take advantage of these kinds of lessons to assist your students in building strategies for reading comprehension and well-organized writing simultaneously.

Genres and Formats

Students must learn to write for many different purposes and audiences. Young children will write for a limited number of purposes as they work to develop their emergent literacy skills. Once they have achieved proficiency with letter-sound associations, their focus will shift to extending and expanding their writing as they become increasingly proficient with written language. Most of their writing will focus on their personal experiences and observations.

As young writers mature, they begin to write for a broader spectrum of purposes. By about second grade, students begin to name genres and distinguish various purposes for writing. Descriptive skills, including strong verbs, onomatopoeia, beginning and ending techniques, and sentence variation will be important at this transitional time, as these skills enhance all genres.

Throughout the intermediate grades, students continue to expand their knowledge and understanding of a growing number of genres and formats. To be effective writing instructors, it's important for teachers to understand the intricacies of each type of writing.

DESCRIPTIVE WRITING

One of the primary tasks for writers in all genres is to help their readers **visualize**. To do this, both expository and narrative writers create imagery through a number of writing-craft techniques. Descriptive pieces are neither narrative nor expository. They are tableaus—frozen scenes inspected in detail by the writer's eye.

Descriptive writing skills must be taught and practiced in a cyclical manner. Continue to revisit them throughout the school year, adding layers of complexity and maturity to each. Develop the vocabulary of description so that when students are writing narrative and expository pieces, you can guide them through revision by naming specific Target Skills that will aid the reader in visualizing the text. Descriptive skills include:

- strong verbs
- descriptive attributes (adjectives associated with a large variety of attributes—color, texture, function, etc.)
- comparisons (comparative and superlative adjectives, similes and metaphors)
- personification
- onomatopoeia
- specificity

Teach and practice descriptive skills in isolation. Then, when composing narrative and expository pieces, your students will have experience with the skills common to each genre.

NARRATIVE

Narratives are stories, characterized by a chronological ordering of events in which people or animals interact in a setting. Time passes in a story. In fiction, the plot drives the story. In personal and informational narrative, the writer's point—**why I am telling you this story**—drives the story.

Writers usually use the past tense for narratives but may occasionally use the present tense. They indicate changes in time and place with transitions such as, *In the afternoon*, or *Meanwhile, back at the ranch*. They also flag these changes, as well as changes of action or speaker, by indenting to form new paragraphs. Narrative writers use engaging beginning and ending techniques and great descriptive imagery to create interesting and entertaining stories.

Some narratives are mainly informational, with the information woven into a chronologically ordered story. Many of Joanna Cole's *The Magic School Bus* books take this form. A book about a family's journey into the Grand Canyon might be crammed full of information about the geology of the canyon. But this informational content does not change the narrative structure of the text: It is still a narrative because it is organized chronologically, with time passing as the text progresses.

Narrative writers use both **genre-specific skills**, such as time transitions or dialogue tags, and **general skills**, such as strong verbs or literary devices. In this section, the various narrative genres are described, followed by the writing-craft skills that are specific to each.

Personal Narrative

Personal narratives are not plot-driven as fiction and plays are. But personal narratives are stories and they do have a point or focus. That point or focus might be an emotion, an accomplishment, a lesson learned, or a reflection about oneself or one's life that derives from the event. Personal narratives are the stories we often cherish and save to tell our grandchildren.

Like all narratives, personal narratives are organized in chronological order. Most have short beginnings and endings and an elaborated middle consisting of a rich description of the main event. Personal narratives are always written in the first person. To enrich their stories, authors often aggrandize them with events and conversations that did not necessarily happen exactly as they relate them. In this regard, William Zinsser titled his book about writing memoir, *Inventing the Truth*.

Children's picture books written in the first person make good models for personal-narrative writing at any grade level. These first-person narratives are not written by children, but the authors have written them from the perspective of their childhoods. Prime examples include Barbara Park's *Junie B. Jones* series and Mercer Mayer's *Little Critter* books.

In kindergarten and first-grade classes, you should read many personal narratives to your students and help them identify and articulate the ending that drives the story—which most often is the author's feelings about the event, or what she accomplished or learned. But do not ask these students to write their own personal narratives until they can sequence events in time order.

Through eighth grade, continue to read personal narratives to your students to reiterate the chronological organization and to show them the elaboration techniques that writer use. Help them identify the ending that drives the story: the author's feeling or something the author achieved or learned, or a reflection about their own lives based on a text-to-self connection. Such books include Mark Teague's *How I Spent My Summer Vacation*, Sharon Creech's *Walk Two Moons* and Kate DiCamillo's *Because of Winn Dixie*.

Fictional Narrative

Fiction stories are plot driven. The main character has a goal to reach and conflicts to resolve. The writer creates tension through plot and through the use of tension devices, such as setbacks and foreshadowing. Stories are organized in a chronological sequence of events but may include flashbacks—scenes that took place at an earlier time.

There are only six basic plot types, but writers often use them in combinations: character with a problem or a goal; character vs. nature; lost and found; good guys vs. bad guys; mystery and solution; boy meets girl. A story may be about a character with a goal but also feature villains trying to thwart the hero. What differs from story to story of the same plot type are the settings; motives; themes; setbacks; tension-building devices; the writer's style, tone, and voice; and most important, the characters.

Successful fiction writers create characters that their readers care about and want to succeed. The writers reveal the personality of the main characters and show how each of them changes over the course of the story. To do this, writers use the technique of description and relate what the characters say, think, and do, as well as what other characters say about them. Classic examples include Robert McCloskey's *Blueberries for Sal*, Don Freeman's *Corduroy* and E. B. White's *Charlotte's Web*.

EXPOSITORY

Expository books fall into many categories and genres. They may be single-concept books about such things as color, shape, shadows, or light. They may be how-to books. They may describe processes such as life cycles of living things and manufacturing, or systems such as the rain cycle and milk production from cow to cup. They may present information through comparison, problem and solution, or cause-and-effect. They may be essays of opinion or persuasion. They may be art- or photo-illustrated. But, what they are not are stories.

Expository text is organized by clumping related information (or ideas and concepts) or by ordering a sequence of steps. The table of contents reveals this clumping or the step sequence. Point that out to your students when you read from these books. Also, point out that authors can, and usually do, put bits of expository text in a story.

Some expository techniques, like comparison, persuasion, and process description, are used by authors of narratives. You can use these books to model the techniques, and students will usually find them very engaging. However, students will most often be required to write non-fiction expository text. Therefore, be sure to keep on hand many non-fiction books and age appropriate magazines to use as literature models. At the end of this book, you will find a matrix listing non-fiction literature models that can be used to demonstrate the application of writing craft Target Skills in non-fiction text.

Informational Expository

Well-written informational expository text is engaging. Its writers achieve this in a number of ways. They use creative hooks and ending techniques. They employ vivid imagery. They talk directly to their readers using the pronouns *you, we, I,* and *us.* They embed definitions of content words in the text so their readers do not have to constantly flip back and forth to the glossary. They present the information in a logically organized form so their readers can easily follow the text.

> **Note:** Science-standards-based guided reading books, which are informational texts often found in "leveled reader" series, are especially useful in teaching ELL students to read. These students' background experiences are considerably more likely to be activated when the topic is weather, animals, plants, water, or rocks; as opposed to magical experiences and talking animals. Informational text about science is almost always culturally neutral.

Expository writing is almost always presented in clumps of related information or ideas. To show how the bits of information relate to each other, writers use a variety of text structures within a piece. These could include description; contrast; comparison; main idea and support; main idea and multiple examples; definition; step order; and cause-and-effect. Informational models include Arthur Durros's *Ant Cities* and Sneed Collard's *Animal Dads*.

Procedural Expository

Directions, or descriptions of procedures or processes, are presented as a list or in running text. When it is list-like, the writer usually uses imperative verbs. List-like text is conventionally bulleted or numbered. For example:

1. Open the seed package.
2. Dig a row of holes in the soil about two inches deep.
3. Place one seed in each hole.
4. Water every day...etc.

Running text makes use of transitions such as *after that, first, next, when,* and *finally* to establish progression:

> *If you want to build a birdhouse, you will need plywood, small nails, a hammer, a saw, and a plan.* **First**, *check your plan to find out how much plywood you need.* **Then**, *using the plan, make pattern pieces from paper and lay them on the plywood. Trace around them.* **Next**, *saw around each pattern piece, cutting it from the plywood...*

Sometimes, process description is embedded within the context of narrative writing, including fiction. In Tomie dePaola's *The Popcorn Book,* the process of popping popcorn is delivered as a counterpoint to the story of two brothers making a snack. In *Everglades*, Jean Craighead George artfully weaves the evolution of an endangered ecosystem into a tale about five children traveling by canoe through the Florida Everglades with an enlightening guide.

Process description is a clever motif used by some fiction authors. The very popular *How to Train Your Dragon* series by Cressida Cowell is an example of procedural motif used as a vehicle for the adventure genre. In the hallmark book of the series, *How to Train Your Dragon (Book 1)*, chapter titles like "First Catch Your Dragon," "Training Your Dragon the Hard Way," and "When Yelling Doesn't Work" engage the reader in the narrative with the hook of procedural language.

There are many examples of books that revolve around the purpose of process description. Gail Gibbons's *From Seed to Plant* is an informational text about plant growth delivered through text and pictures. Nancy Carlson's *How to Lose All Your Friends* is a tongue-in-cheek instruction manual for social behavior, while Laurie Krasny Brown's *How to Be a Friend: A Guide to Making Friends and Keeping Them* takes a more practical and direct approach to creating friendships and resolving conflicts.

The most common procedural text that students probably encounter is a set of directions. When playing games or making crafts, they often follow a set of written steps. When completing a science experiment, students follow a set of procedures. This type of reading is an authentic, functional, real-world task.

When students learn the inverse of the process—when they gain competence and experience writing a set of directions or a process description, such as a science experiment or steps to playing a game or making a craft—they understand the intricacies of the genre from the author's perspective. This understanding builds a cognitive foundation for comprehending procedural text, making the most of the complementary relationship between reading and writing.

Comparison Expository

Comparison is all about presenting similarities and differences. It is an important **critical thinking skill**. Robert Marzano's research (2003) found that of all the instructional strategies that positively affect student achievement, helping students **identify similarities and differences** (in other words, making comparisons) had the largest average positive effect on achievement.

Comparison lies at the heart of analytical thinking. Writing comparison papers is a task students are called upon to do throughout their school careers. To do it successfully, they need to hear and see models of comparison often.

When writing comparison pieces, authors use various text structures to compare two things. In *So You Think You Want to Be President?*, author Judith St. George begins the text with a comparison sentence:

> *"There are good things about being President and there are bad things about being President."*

Sometimes authors use paired sentences to make comparisons. Note the juxtaposition of contrasting details in paired sentences used by Elizabeth Dahlie in her narrative tale, *Bernelly and Harriet: The Country Mouse and the City Mouse*:

> *"Bernelly is a country mouse who spends most of her time outdoors, teaching fly-fishing and tying beautiful flies. Harriet is a city mouse who lives and paints in her cozy apartment in the heart of the city."*

Often, authors write paired paragraphs to make comparisons. In the classic children's book *Blueberries for Sal*, Robert McCloskey used this text structure:

> *" 'We will take our berries home and can them,' said her mother. 'Then we will have food for winter.' Sal's mother walked slowly through the bushes, picking blueberries as she went and putting them in her pail..."*
>
> *"On the other side of Blueberry Hill, Little Bear came with his mother to eat blueberries. 'Little Bear,' she said, 'eat lots of berries and grow big and fat. We must store up food for the long, cold winter.' "*

Analyzing comparison techniques used by authors in both fiction and non-fiction contexts sets the stage for planning comparison writing. Have students read comparison models and create T-charts and Venn diagrams of similarities and differences. These exercises not only aid in comprehension, but also build a foundation for writing.

Persuasive Expository

Writers of persuasive text present an opinion or state their position on an issue and then go on to support it with facts and statistics, logical arguments, comparisons, authoritative quotes, anecdotes, and the like. Children's books do not commonly exemplify persuasive writing craft, so it's important to locate models and make them accessible when teaching this genre of writing.

Judi Barrett states an opinion and uses persuasive arguments as support in her humorous, tongue-in-cheek children's book, *Animals Should Definitely Not Wear Clothing*. Author Denise Fleming takes on a more serious topic in *Where Once There Was a Wood*, using subtle persuasive techniques to move the reader toward conservation efforts. Similarly, Chris Van Allsburg persuades the reader to make personal efforts toward "greener" living through the narrative he creates in *Just a Dream*.

Models of a more direct approach to persuasive writing, the style most often required of students in their writing, can be found in newspapers and children's magazines, like *Ranger Rick* and *National Geographic Kids*. Look for age-appropriate opinion pieces that are relevant to your students in your daily paper. Clip and save them as models to use when teaching persuasive writing. Order magazine subscriptions or encourage your school library to house them and keep them accessible for modeling many forms of non-fiction text, including persuasive writing.

POETRY

Children of all ages enjoy poetry. The beauty of poetry is that it strives to conquer big concepts with a limited number of words. Donald Graves, in his book *Sea of Faces*, chooses to use poetry as a vehicle for getting to know students because, "it can be written quickly and concisely." With poetry, many Target Skills can be succinctly reviewed and applied in a limited amount of time.

A comprehensive collection of children's poetry is an essential tool for a print-rich classroom environment. Look for an anthology with the works of many different poets spanning various types of poetry and an assortment of themes, like *The Random House Book of Poetry for Children*.

Classroom teachers commonly use poetry to teach the concepts of rhythm and rhyme, and poetry units usually include various formats, like haiku and cinquain. However, poetry is teeming with rich examples of Target Skills and can be used as concise literature models.

Christina Rossetti's "Clouds" and Hilda Conkling's "Dandelion" are potent models for teaching metaphor. Margriet Ruurs's "Stagefright" and Eve Merriam's "Willow and Ginkgo" can be used to model simile. At the end of this book, you will find a poetry matrix listing an assortment of easy-to-find poems that can be used as literature models for various Target Skills.

LETTER WRITING

Letter writing is not a separate genre; it is a format for writing. Letters can be narrative, expository, or a mixture of both. When a letter is narrative in nature, its writer tells of events, putting them in chronological order and writing them in the past tense.

> *Dear Nana,*
>
> *Last week my class went to the zoo. I carried the mammal guidebook you gave me for my birthday. When we got to the zoo, we went to the primate house first. (That is where the monkeys and apes are.) We ate lunch right across from the seals. After lunch, my friend Shasta threw up when we were in the reptile house. She was afraid of the lizards. After that, we went into the aviary. Nothing was scary there. We had fun.*
>
> *Love,*
>
> *Kate*

When a letter is purely expository in nature, its writer clumps related facts or ideas and uses present-tense verbs.

> *Dear Nana,*
>
> *I love the mammal guidebook you sent to me for my birthday. So far I have seen twelve different mammals that are in the book. My favorite ones are rodents. You can find them everywhere. Did you know rodents all have the same kind of teeth? They have two big front ones, like a beaver's or a gerbil's. Thank you again for the book.*
>
> *Love,*
>
> *Kate*

Friendly letter conventions, while not written in stone, include salutation and closing formats. Postcards work the same way, though writers often leave off the salutation to have more writing space.

With the advent of e-mail and cell phones, friendly letters are becoming less common—along with clear, grammatical, and well-organized writing. Nonetheless, in spite of this media change, lessons in and practice with writing friendly letters is still relevant.

Some charming children's books model letter formats while providing information or revealing a plot line. Examples include Simon James's *Dear Mr. Blueberry*, Lynne Cherry's *The Armadillo from Amarillo*, and Janet and Allan Ahlberg's *The Jolly Postman*. Additional letter-writing models are listed in the fiction and Spanish literature-model matrices at the end of this book.

A Way of Thinking

Literature models are a vehicle for writing instruction. As you learn to use them, they will become foundational tools in your curriculum. You will become adept at identifying writing craft skills applied in your own reading and you'll begin to think like a writer.

As your students gain fluency with Target Skills and are increasingly exposed to literature models, they will also become critical readers, identifying examples of craft in their independent reading. In other words, your frequent use of literature models will help your students think like writers.

Chapter Three

The Content of Craft

"We'll spend a lifetime crafting our teaching in order to allow children to be the authors of their own texts. We lean into the future striving to be the teachers we envisioned when we first chose the profession."
—Donald Graves

The Craft of Teaching

As teachers, we are dynamic beings. We constantly strive to improve our practice, learning and growing along with our students. We read and listen, we create and experiment. Sometimes we stumble and we make adjustments. But always, we grow and become better at our craft—the craft of teaching.

In this chapter, we will dive into the content of writing—the Target Skills that will support our students in their growth as writers. These skills are the tools of our writing instruction. By closely examining the language of writers and the concepts represented by that language, we will refine our understanding of the craft-based writing curriculum.

Here you will find an alphabetical listing of writing-craft Target Skills. Each skill is defined, its purpose is explored, and an example is provided. An abbreviated list of exemplary literature models is provided for each skill. For your convenience, this book includes a sampling of different types of models, and each is identified as one of the following: Picture Book (PB), Intermediate Text (IT), Poetry (P), or Non-fiction (NF).

Alliteration

Alliteration is the repetition of a beginning sound.

The starlight sang its song of silence, and lulled me off to sleep.

Alliteration is used to produce pleasing sounds, and thus is useful for getting a reader's attention. Avoid misconceptions and clearly communicate that alliteration is the repetition of a sound, not a letter. Alliteration can enhance a theme, establish a rhythm, move the reader quickly along, or create anticipation.

Though we tell young writers not to write incomplete sentences, by fourth grade we can teach them that violating this prohibition can be an effective literary device, as long as it is done by design rather than by mistake. For example, stand-alone phrases, especially alliterative phrases, can produce effective and engaging hooks:

Sipping or slurping. Gripping or grabbing. Clawing or pawing. Animals get their food any way they can.

A sampling of literature models:

A, My Name is Alice by Jane Bayer (PB)
Zipping, Zapping, Zooming Bats by Ann Earle (NF)
Oh, the Places You'll Go! by Dr. Seuss (PB)
"Llook!" by Jack Prelutsky (P)
Some Smug Slug by Pamela Duncan Edwards (PB)

Asides to the Reader

An aside to the reader is a voice technique in which the author digresses from the story to directly address the reader.

Now, dear reader, do not think the story ends here.

Generally used in theatrical pieces, asides occur when the actor's speech is directed toward the audience and is not supposed to be heard by the other actors on stage. Asides are sometimes used by fiction authors to introduce a narrator's voice and share opinions or information. The flow of the narrative is interrupted by a well-placed aside, and the reader feels privy to "insider" information. The reader, being addressed in such a manner, feels more involved in the story and connected to the author.

As young authors gain a mature command of language and demonstrate strong facility with point of view, asides to the reader can be introduced and students can experiment with their use in fictional narratives.

A sampling of literature models:

Bunnicula: A Rabbit-Tale of Mystery by Deborah Howe and James Howe (IT)
The Bad Beginning by Lemony Snicket (IT)
The Tale of Despereaux by Kate DiCamillo (IT)
The Ticky-Tacky Doll by Cynthia Rylant (PB)
Walter the Baker by Eric Carle (PB)

Beginning Technique: Dialogue

Sometimes authors "hook" readers by beginning a piece with words spoken by a character.

"Watch out!" the coach shouted, a little too late.

Dialogue, when used as a beginning technique, can hook the reader by creating the feeling that the action has already begun and the reader is joining the characters in the middle of a scene. In a narrative, true introductory exposition—an introduction to the main character(s), setting, and situation—occurs after the reader has become engaged in the piece.

In expository pieces, a line of dialogue can be used as a compelling beginning hook as well. A quotation from someone associated with the subject of the piece can quickly draw the reader's attention. For instance, "Give me liberty or give me death!" might be used to start a piece about Patrick Henry. Or, the author may quote an expert in the subject of the piece, such as this start of an article about chemistry labs in schools:

"Never use taste as a tool in the chemistry lab," Dr. Graves advises his high school students.

A sampling of literature models:

A Picture Book of Davy Crockett by David Adler (NF)
Daisy and the Egg by Jane Simmons (PB)
"Oh Please Take Me Fishing" by Jack Prelutsky (P)
Sarah, Plain and Tall by Patricia MacLachlan (IT)
The Day Jimmy's Boa Ate the Wash by Trinka Hakes Nobel (PB)

Beginning Technique: Exclamation

Begin a piece with an exclamatory sentence.

Eureka! I finally found a way to get my family to reduce waste by recycling.

Writers use exclamations to show that something exciting is happening, or that a particular fact is exciting to know. The writer hopes that the reader will get excited, too, and want to read on.

Exclamations as beginning techniques can be used in both narrative and expository pieces, and can be used proficiently by primary and intermediate writers.

A sampling of literature models:

"A True Story" by Brod Bagert (P)
Fourth Grade Rats by Jerry Spinelli (IT)
My Hands by Aliki (NF)
Recycle! A Handbook for Kids by Gail Gibbons (NF)
The Underwater Alphabet Book by Jerry Pallotta (PB)

Beginning Technique: Idiom

An idiom is a common figure of speech. Because idioms are commonly understood, an author who begins a piece with an idiom can hook the reader with the familiarity of the phrase and can express a big concept with very few words.

Birds of a feather flock together.

Idioms are figures of speech that act as language shortcuts. They are often metaphoric in nature. The idiom given as an example above is a common expression used to avoid a long explanation about the ways in which two characters are similar. When used as a beginning technique, idioms can give the reader a tacit understanding and the feeling of being a language "insider."

Some people may think that idioms are "a dime a dozen," but "a little bird told me" that children can have lots of fun with them! Author Peggy Parish created her *Amelia Bedelia* books around the idea of idiom and Amelia's literal interpretation of words.

A sampling of literature models:

Amelia and Eleanor Go For a Ride by Pam Muñoz Ryan (PB)
Bringing Ezra Back by Cynthia DeFelice (IT)
Clifford, We Love You by Norman Bridwell (PB)
The World is Your Oyster by Tamara James (PB)

Beginning Technique: Introduction of the Main Character

Authors often begin a piece by naming the character central to the story.

Sam Johnson was an eight-year-old magician.

People like to read about people. Authors take advantage of that by naming a character central to a story or informational piece as a hook technique.

A story or an expository piece can start with a description of the essential or predominant traits of the most important character or person in the piece. The description need only be as long as it takes to engage the reader.

A sampling of literature models:

Because of Winn-Dixie by Kate DiCamillo (IT)
Big Anthony and the Magic Ring by Tomie dePaola (PB)
Henry and Beezus by Beverly Cleary (IT)
My Great-Aunt Arizona by Gloria Houston (PB)
Sylvester and the Magic Pebble by William Steig (PB)

Beginning Technique: Onomatopoeia

The term onomatopoeia refers to words created to imitate sounds. When used as a beginning technique, onomatopoeia is an immediate attention-getter.

Thwack! *My eyes were closed when the bat finally connected with the ball.*

Onomatopoeia is a type of sensory language, imitating sounds so that the reader can imagine hearing them. It can heighten the reader's involvement in a piece, thus engaging the reader.

If a writer uses onomatopoeia as a beginning hook, naturally the sound has to be associated with the topic. If the writer starts with *BZZZZZZ*, the reader expects to read about bees or hummingbirds, or something that buzzes.

A sampling of literature models:

A House of Tailors by Patricia Reilly Giff (IT)
Berlioz the Bear by Jan Brett (PB)
Bridge to Terabithia by Katherine Paterson (IT)
The Lion and the Mouse by Jerry Pinkney (PB)
The Little Engine That Could by Watty Piper (PB)

Beginning Technique: Question

In a question hook, the author talks directly to readers, asking a question designed to pique their interest in the subject. Authors may also begin pieces by posing a question within a line of dialogue.

Have you ever tried to hold a conversation with a frog?

Question hooks automatically invite the reader into a thought process. They indirectly stimulate prior experience and background knowledge, engaging the reader and setting the context for the book.

Question hooks are often used in non-fiction text because of their power to access prior knowledge. Questions are also used as beginning techniques in many children's books, giving the child a sense of assumed familiarity with the author.

A sampling of literature models:

Ant Cities by Arthur Dorros (NF)
Charlotte's Web by E. B. White (IT)
Digging Up Dinosaurs by Aliki (NF)
Do You Want to Be My Friend? by Eric Carle (PB)
"What is Poetry? Who Knows?" by Eleanor Farjeon (P)

Beginning Technique: Setting

Authors sometimes hook the reader by beginning a piece with an indication or description of the time and/or place in which the book is set.

It was a dark and stormy night in the little town of Winston. The only sound was the rustling of leaves in the slow-moving wind and the occasional hiss of an alley cat.

Writers of stories and expository sometimes use setting to start their pieces. They describe time or place in a creative way to capture the reader's interest.

Visual details generate the reader's involvement by stimulating the imagination with pictures. Modern students are accustomed to elaborate settings on television, in movies, and even in video games. Well-written setting descriptions can be very effective beginning techniques.

A sampling of literature models:

A Picture Book of Lewis and Clark by David A. Adler (NF)
Farmer Boy by Laura Ingalls Wilder (IT)
Night in the Country by Cynthia Rylant (PB)
The Lorax by Dr. Seuss (PB)
Verdi by Janell Cannon (PB)

Clues for Inference

Authors paint "word pictures," allowing readers to put details together to form their own conclusions, rather than the author making direct statements.

Her mouth was drawn down on each end, and a small tear formed in the corner of one eye.

Good readers **think**, and good writers stimulate them to do it. They do this by not telling their readers everything. Instead, they leave clues so the readers have to figure out some things for themselves.

Rather than writing "dinky" sentences that "hit the reader over the head," skilled authors weave clues into their descriptions that allow the reader to infer meaning. Incorporating clues for inference boosts the quality of writing and can yield reciprocal benefits with implicit reading comprehension for all students—especially English-language learners and struggling readers.

A sampling of literature models:

Happy Birthday, Moon by Frank Asch (PB)
Hatchet by Gary Paulsen (IT)
"I Heard a Bird Sing" by Oliver Herford (P)
Two Bad Ants by Chris Van Allsburg (PB)
Wanted...Mud Blossom by Betsy Byars (IT)

Descriptive Attributes

The substance of description is made up of attributes, including size, shape, color, texture, number, and sensory attributes.

*His **worn, hardwood** cane was about **three feet long** and covered with **alternating dark and light brown wood-grain** stripes running the length of its **smooth** surface.*

Attributes are the properties of physical elements perceived through the five senses. They are observed directly, remembered from experience, or imagined. For the most part, we use adjectives to qualify and quantify these attributes.

Adjectives can describe sensory attributes, such as color, texture, smell, taste, age, and size, with very specific vocabulary (*purple, smooth, acrid, bitter, ten-year-old, fourteen-inch*). Other adjectival vocabulary is non-specific (*small, young*) or comparative (*as green as a lime, like licorice, satiny*). Teach students to describe visual images without creating list-like sentences containing an overabundance of adjectives.

A sampling of literature models:

"Cereal" by Shel Silverstein (P)
Charlotte's Web by E. B. White (IT)
Goodnight Moon by Margaret Wise Brown (PB)
Mrs. Piggle-Wiggle by Betty MacDonald (IT)
My Father's Hands by Joanne Ryder (PB)

Dialogue Tags

Dialogue tags are clauses added to a line of dialogue in order to identify the speaker. They consist of two main parts—a verb and a speaker's name.

"Please follow me," ***the nurse said****.*

An overuse of dialogue can cause a reader to become detached from text. However, dialogue used sparingly and appropriately can help move the plot along while revealing information about the characters.

The most common verb used in dialogue tags is *said*, but there are many other choices. Writers select words carefully, always considering the rhythm of language and the effectiveness of communication. Demonstrate the use of various dialogue tags in literature, and point out the ways authors move the plot and reveal character traits through well-selected dialogue tags.

Compare the following options to the example above and note the way they change the tone of the dialogue and the characterization of the nurse:

"Please follow me," the nurse whispered hastily.

"Please follow me," the nurse barked in a monotone voice.

"Please follow me," begged the nurse.

The nurse grabbed Dr. Jones by the arm and shouted, "Please follow me!"

A cautionary note: using a different tag on every line of dialogue does not constitute well-crafted writing. If students are choosing creative tags, make sure they are purposeful and effective. Remind students that their primary purpose is to tell the story or inform the reader.

Provide examples of well-written dialogue that is purposeful and effective, containing dialogue tags that help move the plot or reveal information about characters.

A sampling of literature models:

Bud, Not Buddy by Christopher Paul Curtis (IT)
Chrysanthemum by Kevin Henkes (PB)
Jumanji by Chris Van Allsburg (PB)
Pirates Don't Change Diapers by Melinda Long (PB)
The Tale of Desperaux by Kate DiCamillo (IT)

Embedded Definition

Embedded definitions are the meanings of words or concepts presented within the text. They are most often used in non-fiction, but are sometimes used in fiction as well.

Soon enough, the horse learned to canter, a smooth gait that is faster than a trot but slower than a gallop.

Readers often learn the meanings of new words and concepts through text. Sometimes, the meaning is implicit. However, sometimes writers intentionally place a definition within the flow of the text so that the fluency of the passage is not interrupted.

Fiction authors occasionally embed definitions to build characters or lay a foundation for an event in the plot. Non-fiction authors often present information through definition, devoting one or several sentences to defining a word or concept.

A sampling of literature models:

Sam, Bangs & Moonshine by Evaline Ness (PB)
The Ersatz Elevator by Lemony Snicket (IT)
The Magic School Bus Inside the Earth by Joanna Cole (NF)
The Milk Makers by Gail Gibbons (NF)
When is a Planet Not a Planet?: The Story of Pluto by Elaine Scott (NF)

Ending Technique: Advice to the Reader

The author ends the piece with a recommendation for the reader to follow.

Take it from me, the next time you plan a vacation, consider a camping expedition in the heart of a national park.

Writers of fiction and non-fiction often have a final word of advice for the reader. Fables end with a "moral of the story," which is often advice. Informational text writers sometimes use this ending technique to summarize information or recommend a "next step" in the reader's learning process. Even personal narratives sometimes reiterate the main point of the piece by closing with a recommendation to the reader.

Endings that offer advice add voice to a piece and leave the reader feeling connected to the text and thinking about a way to apply the theme of information presented in their own lives.

A sampling of literature models:

Ant Cities by Arthur Dorros (NF)

"Be Glad Your Nose is on Your Face" by Jack Prelutsky (P)

Check It Out!: The Book about Libraries by Gail Gibbons (NF)

Little Red Riding Hood: A Newfangled Prairie Tale by Lisa Campbell Ernst (PB)

So You Want to be President? by Judith St. George (NF)

Ending Technique: Circle Back to the Hook

Circle back to the hook means using a technique at the end that is similar to the one used at the beginning.

Beginning: *The day the package arrived began like any ordinary day.*

Ending: *The day the package arrived began like any ordinary day, but it turned into the most extraordinary day ever.*

Repeating the form of the hook is an effective way to wrap up a piece and give the reader a feeling of completeness. If the beginning of the piece hooks the reader by asking a question, the end might repeat the question and offer an answer. Sometimes the hook is merely echoed and not directly repeated, but still the reader feels that the story has come full circle.

Endings that circle back to the hook are particularly abundant in magazine articles. As you find them, keep a file of exemplary models to share with your students. Many picture books for young readers also employ this ending technique.

A sampling of literature models:

Comet's Nine Lives by Jan Brett (PB)
If You Give a Mouse a Cookie by Laura Joffe Numeroff (PB)
"I Heard a Bird Sing" by Oliver Herford (P)
I Loved You Before You Were Born by Anne Bowen (PB)
Ox-Cart Man by Donald Hall (PB)

Ending Technique: Feeling Statement

A feeling statement is an efficient way to bring a conclusion to a brief piece.

I was so embarrassed.

Feeling statements are widely taught to young children who write about personal experiences but struggle to bring these pieces to a satisfying conclusion. Because this ending technique is brief and personal, young children can easily learn to apply it to their writing. A first grader can easily end a piece about a special day with a sentence like, "I had so much fun at Disney World."

This ending technique is not often found in trade books. However, personal narrative magazine articles and personal experience poetry often use feeling statements as a succinct way to summarize the author's perspective.

A sampling of literature models:

"April Rain Song" by Langston Hughes (P)
"Flowers are a Silly Bunch" by Arnold Spilka (P)
"Mice" by Rose Fyleman (P)
"Mud" by Polly Chase Boyden (P)
"Night Creature" by Lilian Moore (P)

Ending Technique: Question

Question endings lead readers toward introspection, asking them to think about the main idea of the book or their connection to that idea.

Young Nicholas knew that he had finally found his treasure—in the pages of a book. Where will you find your treasure?

Question endings act as an open invitation to the readers to learn more or to apply what they have learned in the book to future experiences. The question might also serve as a very short summary of the main idea.

Question endings are generally easy for children to learn to write and are appropriate for young writers. Read several literature models that demonstrate well-written question endings that lead the reader into critical thinking.

A sampling of literature models:

Clifford, We Love You by Norman Bridwell (PB)
Dogs Don't Wear Sneakers by Laura Joffe Numeroff (PB)
"Forgotten Language" by Shel Silverstein (P)
My Hands by Aliki (NF)
The Cat in the Hat by Dr. Seuss (PB)

Ending Technique: Remind the Reader

A reminder to the reader is a technique writers use to summarize their main ideas.

Remember that while the porcupine will not "throw" its quills at you, do not try to pick one up. The barbs on the quills make them very difficult to pull out.

This ending technique is most often used in non-fiction writing to summarize the most important points the author is trying to make. However, it can also be used in fiction texts as a way to leave the reader with a message presented in the story.

A sampling of literature models:

My Visit to the Aquarium by Aliki (NF)
It's a Good Thing There Are Insects by Allan Fowler (NF)
The Cloud Book by Tomie dePaola (PB)
So That's How the Moon Changes Shape! by Allan Fowler (NF)
Super-Completely and Totally the Messiest by Judith Viorst (PB)

Ending Technique: Universal Word

Authors sometimes craft conclusions that begin with a universal word, such as *every, all, we, always,* or *everyone.*

***Everybody** needs love.*

The universal-word ending technique uses a word in the last sentence or two that is all encompassing—such as *all the world, everyone, everywhere,* etc. These words create a generalizing statement that summarizes the author's feelings about the subject or states the overall thought the writer wants the reader to take away.

A sampling of literature models:

A. Lincoln and Me by Louise Borden (PB)
"Hug-a-War" by Shel Silverstein (P)
So You Want to be President? by Judith St. George (NF)
Sylvester and the Magic Pebble by William Steig (PB)
Wackiest White House Pets by Kathryn Gibbs Davis (NF)

Hyperbole refers to a figure of speech that uses exaggeration for emphasis or effect.

I've been to Disney World ***millions*** *of times!*

Hyperbole is purposeful exaggeration used to emphasize a point. To say, "*His shoes must be size 48!*" is a creative way of expressing the idea that the subject's feet are big. The reader infers the message without being directly told, understanding that the exaggeration is not meant to be taken literally.

While hyperbole is not appropriate in more formal styles of writing, it can add a whimsical, creative touch and some engaging voice to many narratives. Tall tales are teeming with exaggeration, and it is fun to explore this genre after learning about hyperbole.

A sampling of literature models:

"A Pizza the Size of the Sun" by Jack Prelutsky (P)
Dear Mrs. LaRue: Letters from Obedience School by Mark Teague (PB)
Earrings! by Judith Viorst (PB)
Little Red Cowboy Hat by Susan Lowell (PB)
Sally Ann Thunder Ann Whirlwind Crockett by Steven Kellogg (PB)

Letter Formats

Letter writing is a format of writing, rather than a craft skill.

Friendly letters can be narrative, expository, or a mixture of both. When a letter is narrative in nature, its writer tells of events, putting them in chronological order and writing them in the past tense. For example:

Dear Nana,

Last week my class went to the zoo. I carried the mammal guidebook you gave me for my birthday. When we got to the zoo, we went to the primate house first. After lunch, my friend Shasta threw up when we were in the reptile house! She was afraid of the lizards. After that, we went into the aviary. Nothing was scary there. We had fun.

Love, Kate

When a letter is purely expository in nature, its writer clumps related facts or ideas and uses present-tense verbs. For example:

Dear Nana,

I love the mammal guidebook you sent to me for my birthday. So far I have seen twelve different mammals that are in the book. My favorite ones are rodents. Did you know rodents all have the same kind of teeth? Two big front ones, like a beaver's or gerbil's. Thank you again for the book.

Love, Kate

Friendly letter conventions, while not written in stone, include salutation and closing formats. Postcards work the same way, though writers often leave off the salutation to have more writing space.

With the advent of e-mail and text messaging, friendly letters are somewhat a thing of the past. Nonetheless, in spite of this media change, lessons in and practice with this writing format are still relevant.

A sampling of literature models:

Dear Mr. Blueberry by Simon James (PB)

Dear Mr. Henshaw by Beverly Cleary (IT)

Dear Mrs. LaRue: Letters from Obedience School by Mark Teague (PB)

Hattie Big Sky by Kirby Larson (IT)

Letters from Rifka by Karen Hesse (IT)

Metaphor

A metaphor is a comparison of two unlike things—calling one item or concept by another name—to help the reader build understanding by forming a visual image.

The hurdler became a gazelle, popping over the hurdles without a falter.

A metaphor highlights an attribute of something by calling it something else that is a prime example of that attribute. Thus, even though the writer does not explicitly identify this attribute, the reader is able to infer it.

Some examples will clarify the concept: Call someone an *ox* and the reader will infer *strength*. Call someone a *shrimp* and the reader will infer *small*. Using the term *weasel* usually implies *sneakiness*, while *lion* implies *bravery*.

A sampling of literature models:

Canoe Days by Gary Paulsen (IT)
"Clouds" by Christina Rossetti (P)
From the Mixed-Up Files of Mrs. Basil E. Frankweiler by E. L. Konisburg (IT)
In November by Cynthia Rylant (PB)
Night in the Barn by Faye Gibbons (PB)

Onomatopoeia

Onomatopoeia refers to words created to imitate sounds.

Vroom, vroom*. The car started immediately when I turned the key.*

As discussed earlier, onomatopoeia can be an effective a beginning technique. However, onomatopoeia can also be used throughout a piece to maintain the reader's attention, add sentence variation, and identify a specific sound.

Onomatopoeia is the use of words that when spoken imitate a sound. They might be real words or they may be words created to mimic sound effects. This sound is related to the topic and creates a multi-sensory effect. Such sensory language is powerful in its ability to prompt the reader to connect with the text.

Writers use creative phonetic spelling to write some of the sounds. There are some commonly used spellings, like *vroom* and *whack*. Others are created by the author to create the desired effect.

A sampling of literature models:

Country Crossing by Jim Aylesworth (PB)
"Pie Problem" by Shel Silverstein (P)
Night in the Barn by Faye Gibbons (PB)
Stellaluna by Janell Cannon (PB)
Tom by Tomie dePaola (PB)

Personification

Personification means giving human qualities to non-living or non-human objects.

The leaves danced across the lawn while the trees flung their branches this way and that.

Personification attributes people-like characteristics to inanimate objects. It is therefore a kind of comparison, like a metaphor. Personification is an effective descriptive technique, helping the reader visualize and connect with text.

Because personification is a type of figurative language, both creating and interpreting it require higher-order thinking skills. Putting your students in the writer's seat and having them use personification in their written pieces will yield wonderful reciprocal benefits as they strive to interpret and comprehend figurative language in text.

A sampling of literature models:

Crispin: Cross of Lead by Avi (IT)
"Night" by Mary Ann Hoberman (P)
"Fog" by Carl Sandburg (P)
Red Sings from Treetops: A Year in Colors by Joyce Sidman (PB)
White Snow, Bright Snow by Alvin Tresselt (PB)

Repetition

Repetition occurs when authors repeat words, phrases, or sentences.

First he ate ***all of the*** *carrots, then* ***all of the*** *lettuce, and as if that wasn't enough, he ate* ***all of the*** *squash!*

Repetition is frequently used in poetry, often used in narrative writing, and sometimes used in expository writing.

Writers use repetition for two main reasons. First, the repeated word, phrase, or sentence can be emphasized by being restated. Another reason for using repetition is aesthetic. Authors may like the sound of the repeated words. Repetition can sometimes establish rhythm in a piece of writing, and can add a sense of comfortable predictability for the reader.

A sampling of literature models:

"April Rain Song" by Langston Hughes (P)
"I Am Running in a Circle" by Jack Prelutsky (P)
Millions of Cats by Wanda Gág (PB)
Nocturne by Jane Yolen (PB)
When I Was Young in the Mountains by Cynthia Rylant (PB)

Rhyme

Rhyme is the repetition of the middle and ending sounds of words.

His plans are nothing but ***pie*** *in the* ***sky****!*

Rhyme is often associated with poetry. While not all poems include rhyme, poetry is definitely the genre in which rhyme is used most often. Rhyming words give a lighthearted feel to a piece and can create a pattern with sounds.

For emergent readers, rhyming texts offer predictability through sound patterns, supporting young students working to acquire the word-recognition skills needed to read connected text. Exploring word families can help these students build decoding skills.

Intermediate readers can analyze rhyme patterns in poetry and can easily understand that rhyme is dependent upon the repetition of **sounds**, not **spellings**. For these students, rhyme can be modeled and applied as a vehicle for creating mood and supporting meaning.

A sampling of literature models:

A House Is a House for Me by Mary Ann Hoberman (PB)
"A Remarkable Adventure" by Jack Prelutsky (P)
Chicka Chicka Boom Boom by Bill Martin, Jr. and John Archambault (PB)
"Sick" by Shel Silverstein (P)
Nocturne by Jane Yolen (PB)

Sentence Variation

Writers intentionally vary the form and length of sentences within a piece.

I stopped. I turned slowly around. Was it just my imagination? Suddenly, something dropped from the shelf and landed in front of me, creating a cloud of dust. Eek!

Writers need to keep their readers engaged. A good way to achieve this is through sentence variation. Gary Provost, in his classic non-fiction writing guide, *100 Ways to Improve Your Writing*, cleverly illustrates what happens when writers do not vary sentence length:

This sentence has five words. Here are five more words. Five-word sentences are fine. But several together become monotonous. Listen to what is happening. The writing is getting boring. The sound of it drones. It's like a stuck record.

Young writers can vary the length of their sentences by adding phrases and clauses to extend a sentence (to provide more information or detail); by constructing compound sentences; or by beginning sentences with transitions or occasionally conjunctions. Teach young writers that such techniques will help them keep their readers awake.

A sampling of literature models:

An Octopus Is Amazing by Patricia Lauber (NF)
Because of Winn-Dixie by Kate DeCamillo (IT)
Loser, by Jerry Spinelli (IT)
Rain by Robert Kalan (NF)
Stellaluna by Janell Cannon (PB)

Simile

A simile uses the words *like* or *as* to compare two unlike entities or objects

He ran away ***as*** *fast* ***as*** *a bolt of lightning, his image vanishing* ***like*** *a magician's rabbit.*

A simile is a literary device used to create imagery through comparison. Authors use similes to compare one thing to another based on a single common attribute. Similes use the format *as...as...* (*as* clear *as* glass) or *like a...* (walking mechanically, *like a* robot) to compare two things.

While similes can be very effective in helping the reader create visual images, they can become distracting if overused. Teach students to use similes sparingly so that their effectiveness is preserved. Also teach students to avoid similes that have been used so often that they fail to conjure a mental image (*as fast as a cheetah*). Fresh, original similes should be encouraged.

A sampling of literature models:

Quick as a Cricket by Audrey Wood (PB)
Bud Barkin, Private Eye by James Howe (IT)
Snow by Cynthia Rylant (PB)
"Stagefright" by Margriet Ruurs (P)
"Willow and Ginkgo" by Eve Merriam (P)

Specificity

Specificity refers to the use of specific common and proper nouns.

We went to Target and selected tulips from its garden center.

Good readers make text-to-self connections. An important way by which authors help them do this is through a writing-craft technique called specificity. Specificity means writing *Target* instead of *store* and *tulips* instead of *flowers*. By using specificity, you make your readers smile as they say to themselves, "Oh, that's just like me! I have been there, too!"

Because specificity sometimes involves the use of proper nouns, it also creates a great opportunity for reinforcing the rules of capitalization or providing a good revision tool for young writers.

A sampling of literature models:

"Alexander's Breakfast" by Brod Bagert (P)
Chester's Way by Kevin Henkes (PB)
Nothing Ever Happens on 90th Street by Roni Schotter (PB)
Plants That Never Bloom by Ruth Heller (NF)
Tales of a Fourth Grade Nothing by Judy Blume (IT)

Strong Verbs

Strong verbs are action verbs that are specific and easily visualized by the reader.

The mockingbird ***swooped*** *and* ***screeched***, ***chasing*** *the hawk away from her nest.*

Good readers visualize. Good writers help them do so by creating imagery. Strong verbs are one of a writer's most powerful imagery tools and, as such, are the most important early Target Skill craft lessons for all writers.

Teach young writers to identify strong verbs in literature and create lists to use as writing resources. Purposely construct sentences containing weak verbs to provide revision practice for your students. Strong verbs can transform a bland piece of writing into lively, engaging text.

A sampling of literature models:

Volcano: The Eruption and Healing of Mount St. Helens by Patricia Lauber (NF)
The Wind Blew by Pat Hutchins (PB)
"Spring" by Karla Kuskin (P)
Everglades by Jean Craighead George (PB)
The Slippery Slope by Lemony Snicket (IT)

Transitions: Place

Place transitions are cues that signal a change in setting or location.

George crept ***downstairs*** *where he could more easily eavesdrop on the conversation.*

Place transitions include words and phrases such as *under the porch*; *across the yard*; *inside the house*; *meanwhile, back at the ranch*; and the like. They are most often found in narratives, where they help the reader follow a character's movements or actions.

Sometimes place transitions are used in expository pieces to guide the reader through changing locations (*When a guest enters the lobby*; *As the troops moved onto the rugged shore*; *His family moved to Boston*; etc.).

Modeling and practicing place transitions can facilitate good revision practice. Have students reread their narratives to make sure they have indicated changes in place or location, and teach students to use changes in location to create new paragraphs in a narrative.

A sampling of literature models:

Ant Cities by Arthur Dorros (NF)

Blueberries for Sal by Robert McCloskey (PB)

"Cats" by Eleanor Farjeon (P)

Stickeen: John Muir and the Brave Little Dog by John Muir, as retold by Donnell Rubay (PB)

The Reptile Room by Lemony Snicket (IT)

Transitions: Time

Time transitions are cues that signal a change in time.

As the sun began to peek above the horizon*, he could no longer wait.*

Time transitions include words and phrases such as *early one morning*, *after lunch*, *at 4:00*, *later that day*, and the like. They are most often found in narratives, where they give order to the reader by showing the passage of time.

Narratives are organized chronologically, so these transitions are milestones along the story's timeline. While time transitions are most often used in narrative pieces, they are also found in procedural writing (*Before adding the flour*; *Once the substance has congealed*; *After 24 hours*; etc.).

Students often overuse the word *then*. Teaching them to replace *then* with a time transition in several spots throughout a piece can be an effective revision activity. Again, teach students that a change in time generally signals a new paragraph.

A sampling of literature models:

"Eat-it-All-Elaine" by Kay Starbird (P)

Martin's Big Words: The Life of Dr. Martin Luther King, Jr. by Doreen Rappaport (NF)

Stickeen: John Muir and the Brave Little Dog by John Muir, as retold by Donnell Rubay (PB)

The Grouchy Ladybug by Eric Carle (PB)

Volcano: The Eruption and Healing of Mount St. Helens by Patricia Lauber (NF)

Voice

Voice is the unique style of an author's language.

Boy, are you in for a surprise. Sit back, get comfortable, and hang on!

Voice is difficult to define precisely. It is made up of many components that together account for the uniqueness of each writer's language—his written fingerprint, if you will. It manifests itself in the words the author chooses, the tone he takes, the way he talks to his reader, the details he presents as important, the imagery he creates, and the rhythm of his writing.

We can teach young writers several specific techniques that will help them develop their voices as they practice writing craft, read well-written text, gain experience, and develop vocabulary. We've already discussed *asides to the reader* as a powerful voice technique. Using pronouns to address the reader is another commonly used voice technique.

As you attempt to model this nebulous craft skill, your most effective method may be to juxtapose literature models that exhibit strong, but different voice techniques. Help students analyze the similarities and differences in the syntax, rhythm, and word choices among these pieces.

A sampling of literature models:

Amelia's Notebook by Marissa Moss (PB)
Possum Come a-Knockin' by Nancy Van Laan (PB)
So You Want to Be President? by Judith St. George (NF)
The Original Adventures of Hank the Cowdog by John R. Erickson (IT)
The True Story of the Three Little Pigs by Jon Scieszka (PB)

Immersing Students in Craft

As your students are exposed to high-quality literature—through their independent reading, your read-alouds, and literature models used during writing instruction—they will realize that craft is everywhere. As you teach students **what writers know** through craft skills, you will awaken their critical thinking skills, and they will begin to recognize craft elements by name.

Keep running lists of craft examples in your classroom. Put them on chart paper and make the lists accessible to students so they can add examples of craft from their own reading. These lists should be fluid and dynamic. Once you have introduced a skill, build and maintain the concept by allowing students to take ownership of lists and feel intangibly rewarded for recognizing craft in their reading.

As students write, you also may want to collect examples of craft from their writing and list them on chart paper, class reward charts, or your website. The excitement will grow and take on its own momentum as your students see craft exploding from the literature that surrounds them.

Chapter Four

Literature-model Matrices

The greatest magic in the land
Are books you hold in your hand.
—Kalli Dakos

How to Use the Matrices

This chapter provides an invaluable resource for teachers of writing. On the next several pages, you will find four separate matrices to help you plan for instruction by easily identifying high-quality literature models for an assortment of writing-craft Target Skills. These pages will help put the right books in your hands to model writing craft for your students.

We know that you have your own literature models that might not be listed here, and we realize that new works for children are continually being published. Therefore, each matrix is followed by an additional page with a blank matrix that you can use to compile your own titles as you locate them.

Each matrix contains a wealth of models, listed in alphabetical order by title. Target Skills are identified in columns at the top of each page. Note that most titles have more than one Target Skill identified, maximizing the use of each literature model.

The models listed cover a wide range of styles, topics, and levels, making them useful in a vast array of classroom environments. Likewise, there are four separate literature-model matrices to address a broad area of need: *fiction*, *non-fiction*, *poetry*, and *Spanish* titles.

About the Fiction Literature-model Matrix

The fiction literature-model matrix contains many well-known picture books and a large number of intermediate texts as well. Remember, you can freely use picture books to demonstrate writing craft at all levels. The text in picture books is generally brief, and skills are easy to locate.

However, you may want to use some intermediate models too. These books often contain mature applications of Target Skills within a substantive context. If you teach older students, these books may be familiar and interesting to them. Therefore, there are many intermediate fiction models listed in this matrix, and they are indicated with an asterisk for easy identification.

Because the length of intermediate texts might hinder your ability to readily locate individual skills, specific chapters are indicated to make your search easier. Keep in mind that writing craft is not limited to the chapters identified on the matrix. Feel free to identify multiple examples of a Target Skill within an intermediate text. Small sticky notes or portable divider tabs can help you mark skills in your chapter books.

FICTION LITERATURE-MODEL MATRIX

FICTION LITERATURE-MODEL MATRIX			BEGINNING TECHNIQUE											ENDING TECHNIQUE																		
Title and Author	ALLITERATION	ASIDES TO THE READER	DIALOGUE	EXCLAMATION	IDIOM	INTRO OF MAIN CHARACTER	ONOMATOPOEIA	QUESTION	SETTING	CLUES FOR INFERENCE	DESCRIPTIVE ATTRIBUTES	DIALOGUE TAGS	EMBEDDED DEFINITION	ADVICE TO THE READER	CIRCLE BACK TO THE HOOK	QUESTION	REMIND THE READER	UNIVERSAL WORD	HYPERBOLE	LETTER FORMATS	METAPHOR	ONOMATOPOEIA	PERSONIFICATION	REPETITION	RHYME	SENTENCE VARIATION	SIMILE	SPECIFICITY	STRONG VERBS	TRANSITIONS: PLACE	TRANSITIONS: TIME	VOICE
A House Is a House for Me, Mary Ann Hoberman	●																							●	●							
A House of Tailors, Patricia Reilly Giff * - Ch. 1							●				●											●				●	●	●				
A Mountain Alphabet, Margriet Ruurs	●																											●	●			
A Pacific Alphabet, Margriet Ruurs	●																								●			●				
A, My Name is Alice, Jane E. Bayer	●																											●				
A. Lincoln and Me, Louise Borden																		●									●	●				
Africa Dream, Eloise Greenfield																								●		●		●	●			●
Alexander and the Terrible, Horrible...Day, Judith Viorst											●															●						●
Alexander and the Wind-Up Mouse, Leo Lionni				●																				●	●	●				●	●	
Amelia And Eleanor Go For A Ride, Pam Muñoz Ryan					●																											
Amelia's Notebook, Marissa Moss		●																											●			●
Amos & Boris, William Steig																								●		●		●				
An Octopus Is Amazing, Patricia Lauber													●													●						
Animals Should Definitely Not Wear Clothing, Judi Barrett											●																	●	●			
As Quick as a Cricket, Audrey Wood	●																							●	●		●					
Because of Winn-Dixie, Kate DiCamillo * – Ch. 1						●				●	●	●														●		●				
Berlioz the Bear, Jan Brett							●					●										●				●			●	●		
Bernelly and Harriet: The City Mouse and the Country Mouse, Elizabeth Dahlie						●																								●		
Big Al, Andrew Clements	●					●																										
Big Anthony and the Magic Ring, Tomie dePaola						●																				●		●	●			
Bigmama's, Donald Crews			●					●			●											●										●
Blueberries for Sal, Robert McCloskey												●										●								●		
Boo to a Goose, Mem Fox											●														●				●			
Brave Irene, William Steig											●	●											●			●			●	●		●
Bridge to Terabithia, Katherine Paterson * - Ch. 1							●															●					●		●			
Bringing Ezra Back, Cynthia DeFelice * - Ch. 1					●							●																	●			●

Brown Bear, Brown Bear, What Do You See?, Eric Carle								●			●													●	●							
Bud Barkin, Private Eye, James Howe * - Ch. 1												●															●		●			●
Bud, Not Buddy, Christopher Paul Curtis * - Ch. 9											●	●									●					●		●	●			●
Bunnicula: A Rabbit-Tale of Mystery, Deborah and James Howe * - Ch. 2		●										●														●		●	●			
Bunny Bungalow, Cynthia Rylant	●	●																						●	●			●	●			●
Bunny Cakes, Rosemary Wells											●	●														●						
Cactus Hotel, Brenda Z. Guiberson									●		●				●							●						●	●			
Canoe Days, Gary Paulsen											●										●								●	●		●
Charlotte's Web, E.B. White * - Ch. 1								●			●	●																	●			
Charlotte's Web, E.B. White * - Ch. 3									●	●	●	●		●												●		●	●	●		●
Charlotte's Web, E. B. White * - Ch. 4										●	●													●		●		●	●		●	
Chester's Way, Kevin Henkes		●				●																						●				
Chicka Chicka Boom Boom, Bill Martin Jr.	●																						●		●							●
Chicken Sunday, Patricia Polacco												●												●		●	●	●				
Chrysanthemum, Kevin Henkes											●																	●				
Clap Your Hands, Lorinda Bryan Cauley																									●				●			
Click, Clack, Moo: Cows That Type, Doreen Cronin	●																			●		●										
Clifford, We Love You, Norman Bridwell					●											●																
Colors! Colores!, Jorge Lujan											●										●		●	●			●		●			
Comet's Nine Lives, Jan Brett						●									●													●		●		
Commotion in the Ocean, Giles Andreae	●																					●			●			●				
Corduroy, Don Freeman						●				●																				●	●	
Country Crossing, Jim Aylesworth									●		●											●							●			
Crispin: The Cross of Lead, Avi * - Ch. 1										●		●											●			●		●	●	●	●	
Crow Boy, Taro Yashima													●									●	●									
Daisy and the Egg, Jane Simmons			●									●																				
Dear Mr. Blueberry, Simon James											●									●									●		●	
Dear Mr. Henshaw, Beverly Cleary										●										●												●
Dear Mrs. LaRue: Letters from Obedience School, Mark Teague											●								●	●						●						●
Detective LaRue: Letters from the Investigation, Mark Teague											●									●						●						●
Does a Kangaroo Have a Mother, Too?, Eric Carle				●											●									●	●							
Dogs Don't Wear Sneakers, Laura Joffe Numeroff																●									●							

FICTION LITERATURE-MODEL MATRIX			BEGINNING TECHNIQUE											ENDING TECHNIQUE																		
Title and Author	ALLITERATION	ASIDES TO THE READER	DIALOGUE	EXCLAMATION	IDIOM	INTRO OF MAIN CHARACTER	ONOMATOPOEIA	QUESTION	SETTING	CLUES FOR INFERENCE	DESCRIPTIVE ATTRIBUTES	DIALOGUE TAGS	EMBEDDED DEFINITION	ADVICE TO THE READER	CIRCLE BACK TO THE HOOK	QUESTION	REMIND THE READER	UNIVERSAL WORD	HYPERBOLE	LETTER FORMATS	METAPHOR	ONOMATOPOEIA	PERSONIFICATION	REPETITION	RHYME	SENTENCE VARIATION	SIMILE	SPECIFICITY	STRONG VERBS	TRANSITIONS: PLACE	TRANSITIONS: TIME	VOICE
Earrings!, Judith Viorst			•																•					•								•
Emma and the Coyote, Margriet Ruurs																													•			
Emma at the Fair, Margriet Ruurs																													•			
Emma's Cold Day, Margriet Ruurs																								•								
Emma's Eggs, Margriet Ruurs																								•								
Esperanza Rising, Pam Muñoz Ryan * - Ch. 1			•							•																•			•			
Everglades, by Jean Craighead George																													•			
Fireflies, Julie Brinckloe									•		•								•		•		•	•		•	•		•			
Flossie and the Fox, Pat McKissack			•	•								•																	•			•
Flower Garden, Eve Bunting								•			•																					
Fourth Grade Rats, Jerry Spinelli * - Ch. 1				•								•														•			•	•	•	
Froggy Bakes a Cake, Jonathan London												•																			•	
Froggy Gets Dressed, Jonathan London												•										•										
Froggy Goes to the Doctor, Jonathan London																						•				•			•			
Froggy Learns to Swim, Jonathan London																						•							•			•
From the Mixed-up Files of Mrs. Basil E. Frankweiler, E.L. Konigsburg * - Ch.1						•					•										•					•		•	•		•	
Galimoto, Karen Lynn Williams												•																•				•
Going West, Jean Van Leeuwen		•																						•		•		•				
Goodnight Moon, Margaret Wise Brown											•							•						•	•							
Grandfather's Journey, Allen Say						•					•																	•				
Hailstones and Halibut Bones, Mary O'Neill											•										•		•	•	•							
Happy Birthday, Moon, Frank Asch	•									•		•																	•		•	
Harriet, You'll Drive Me Wild!, Mem Fox						•																		•								
Hatchet, Gary Paulsen * - Ch. 10										•	•															•			•			
Hattie Big Sky, Kirby Larson * - Ch. 1										•	•	•								•						•		•	•	•	•	
Hello, Ocean, Pam Muñoz Ryan	•										•				•						•		•		•				•			

Henry and Beezus, Beverly Cleary * - Ch. 1						●					●	●																●	●			
Hey! Get Off Our Train, John Burningham			●																					●								
Hey, Al, Arthur Yorinks											●	●																			●	
How I Became a Pirate, Melinda Long																																●
How I Learned Geography, Uri Shulevitz																										●			●	●		
How to Be a Friend: A Guide to Making Friends and Keeping Them, Laurie Krasny Brown																										●			●			●
How to Lose All Your Friends, Nancy Carlson																																●
Hurricane, David Wiesner			●																										●			
Hush! A Thai Lullaby, Mingfong Ho																						●		●	●							●
I Loved You Before You Were Born, Anne Bowen											●				●																	●
I Wish I Were a Butterfly, James Howe											●				●													●				
If You Give a Moose a Muffin, Laura Numeroff															●																	●
If You Give a Mouse a Cookie, Laura Numeroff															●																	●
If You Give a Pig a Pancake, Laura Numeroff															●																	●
In My Backyard, Margriet Ruurs	●										●														●				●			
In November, Cynthia Rylant	●								●		●										●		●	●		●	●					
Is Your Mama a Llama?, Deborah Guarino			●					●		●														●	●							
It's Winter, Linda Glaser											●																		●			
James and the Giant Peach, Roald Dahl * - Ch. 1		●									●	●																●	●			●
Jumanji, Chris Van Allsburg			●								●	●																	●			
Just a Dream, Chris Van Allsburg						●					●	●																●	●	●	●	
Knuffle Bunny: A Cautionary Tale, Mo Willems											●	●										●				●			●	●		
Last Summer with Maizon, Jacqueline Woodson * - Ch. 1										●	●	●											●						●			
Letters From Rifka, Karen Hesse *																				●												
Library Lil, Suzanne Williams	●					●													●								●		●		●	●
Like a Windy Day, Frank and Devin Asch											●																●		●			●
Little Quack, Lauren Thompson	●																					●										
Little Red Cowboy Hat, Susan Lowell						●						●							●							●						●
Little Red Riding Hood: A Newfangled Prairie Tale, Lisa C. Ernst						●								●															●			
Long Night Moon, Cynthia Rylant											●										●		●	●			●					
Loser, Jerry Spinelli * - Ch. 1																									●	●			●			●
Mack Made Movies, Don Brown	●					●									●													●	●			

FICTION LITERATURE-MODEL MATRIX

FICTION LITERATURE-MODEL MATRIX																Ending Technique									Beginning Technique							
Title and Author	Voice	Transitions: Time	Transitions: Place	Strong Verbs	Specificity	Simile	Sentence Variation	Rhyme	Repetition	Personification	Onomatopoeia	Metaphor	Letter Formats	Hyperbole	Universal Word	Remind the Reader	Question	Circle Back to the Hook	Advice to the Reader	Embedded Definition	Dialogue Tags	Descriptive Attributes	Clues for Inference	Setting	Question	Onomatopoeia	Intro of Main Character	Idiom	Exclamation	Dialogue	Asides to the Reader	Alliteration
Make Way for Ducklings, Robert McCloskey					●																●											
Mama Cat Has Three Kittens, Denise Fleming				●																												
Many Luscious Lollipops, Ruth Heller								●														●										
Mice Squeak, We Speak, Tomie dePaola				●				●			●																					
Mike Fink, Steven Kellogg				●										●													●					
Mike Mulligan and His Steam Shovel, Virginia Burton									●	●												●					●					
Millions of Cats, Wanda Gág		●	●						●												●	●										
Mirandy and Brother Wind, Pat McKissack	●																				●	●										
Miss Nelson is Missing!, Harry Allard				●																	●	●	●	●								
Miss Rumphius, Barbara Cooney		●		●																		●					●					
Morning, Noon, and Night, Jean Craighead George		●		●	●													●				●										
Mrs. Mack, Patricia Polacco					●																●		●									
My Father's Hands, Joanne Ryder	●			●																		●										
My Great-Aunt Arizona, Gloria Houston					●		●		●															●			●					
Nasty, Stinky Sneakers, Eve Bunting * - Ch. 1							●														●											
Night in the Barn, Faye Gibbons				●							●	●																		●		
Night in the Country, Cynthia Rylant				●						●	●	●												●								
Nocturne, Jane Yolen				●		●			●	●		●												●								●
Nothing Ever Happens on 90th Street, Roni Schotter				●	●																	●					●					●
Off We Go!, Jane Yolen								●	●		●				●																	●
Oh, the Places You'll Go!, Dr. Seuss	●			●				●	●										●										●			●
Old Black Fly, Jim Aylesworth	●			●	●			●	●																							
On Monday When It Rained, Cherryl Kachenmeister							●															●	●									
Owl Moon, Jane Yolen	●			●			●		●	●	●	●		●								●		●								●
Ox-Cart Man, Donald Hall		●	●		●				●									●														
Paddle-to-the-Sea, Holling Clancy Holling		●			●		●			●											●	●		●								
Pancakes, Pancakes!, Eric Carle																										●						

Pecos Bill, Steven Kellogg																			●										●			●
Pirates Don't Change Diapers, Melinda Long												●														●						●
Polar Bear, Polar Bear, What Do You Hear?, Bill Martin Jr																								●	●				●			
Possum Come a-Knockin', Nancy Van Laan																								●	●				●			●
Racoons and Ripe Corn, Jim Arnosky															●											●			●		●	
Ramona the Pest, Beverly Cleary * - Ch. 1			●								●	●														●			●			
Roxaboxen, Alice McLerran									●		●																	●	●			
Sally Ann Thunder Ann Whirlwind Crockett, Steven Kellogg												●							●								●		●			●
Sarah, Plain and Tall, Patricia MacLachlan * - Ch. 1			●								●	●											●			●	●		●			●
Shades of Black, Sandra L. Pinkney											●										●											
Snow, Cynthia Rylant											●												●			●	●					
Some Smug Slug, Pamela Duncan Edwards	●										●																●		●			
Song and Dance Man, Karen Ackerman						●					●	●			●														●			
Stellaluna, Janell Cannon									●		●	●										●				●	●		●	●		
Stickeen: John Muir and the Brave Little Dog, by John Muir, retold by Donnell Rubay											●	●	●													●			●	●	●	
Strega Nona, Tomie dePaola						●					●													●	●			●	●	●	●	
Stuart Little, E.B. White * - Ch. 1						●					●															●		●	●			
Super-completely and Totally the Messiest, Judith Viorst						●											●							●								
Swimmy, Leo Lionni											●										●					●	●		●			
Sylvester and the Magic Pebble, William Steig						●												●												●	●	
Tacky the Penguin, Helen Lester						●					●											●		●								
Tales of a Fourth Grade Nothing, Judy Blume * - Ch. 1											●	●														●		●		●	●	●
Tar Beach, Faith Ringgold																							●		●			●	●			●
The Amazing Bone, William Steig																							●						●			
The Armadillo from Amarillo, Lynne Cherry													●							●				●				●	●			
The Bad Beginning, Lemony Snicket * - Ch. 1		●								●	●	●	●													●			●			●
The Biggest Bear, Lynd Ward									●									●														
The Carrot Seed, Ruth Krauss																								●							●	
The Cat in the Hat, Dr. Seuss																●								●	●							
The Cloud Book, Tomie dePaola											●						●									●						
The Day Jimmy's Boa Ate the Wash, Trinka Hakes Nobel			●																							●		●	●			
The Ersatz Elevator, Lemony Snicket * - Ch. 1		●								●		●	●															●				●

FICTION LITERATURE-MODEL MATRIX

FICTION LITERATURE-MODEL MATRIX			BEGINNING TECHNIQUE											ENDING TECHNIQUE																		
Title and Author	ALLITERATION	ASIDES TO THE READER	DIALOGUE	EXCLAMATION	IDIOM	INTRO OF MAIN CHARACTER	ONOMATOPOEIA	QUESTION	SETTING	CLUES FOR INFERENCE	DESCRIPTIVE ATTRIBUTES	DIALOGUE TAGS	EMBEDDED DEFINITION	ADVICE TO THE READER	CIRCLE BACK TO THE HOOK	QUESTION	REMIND THE READER	UNIVERSAL WORD	HYPERBOLE	LETTER FORMATS	METAPHOR	ONOMATOPOEIA	PERSONIFICATION	REPETITION	RHYME	SENTENCE VARIATION	SIMILE	SPECIFICITY	STRONG VERBS	TRANSITIONS: PLACE	TRANSITIONS: TIME	VOICE
The Gardener, Sarah Stewart										●										●												●
The Gingerbread Baby, Jan Brett									●													●		●	●				●			
The Giving Tree, Shel Silverstein						●																	●	●							●	
The Great Kapok Tree, Lynne Cherry																						●										
The Grouchy Ladybug, Eric Carle									●		●	●			●													●	●	●	●	
The Hat, Jan Brett	●																					●							●			
The Important Book, Margaret Wise Brown											●													●				●	●			
The Jolly Postman, Janet and Allan Ahlberg																				●					●					●		
The Library Mouse, Daniel Kirk						●					●															●		●	●			
The Lion and the Mouse, Jerry Pinkney							●																									
The Little Engine That Could, Watty Piper							●															●	●	●				●				
The Lorax, Dr. Seuss									●									●						●	●					●	●	●
The Mitten, Jan Brett	●					●					●													●		●	●	●	●	●		
The Moon Book, Gail Gibbons	●																															
The Mud Pony, Caron Lee Cohen						●				●																				●	●	
The Night Before Christmas, Clement Moore										●														●	●			●		●	●	
The Original Adventures of Hank the Cowdog, John R. Erickson *						●																				●						●
The Polar Express, Chris Van Allsburg										●	●															●			●			
The Popcorn Book, Tomie dePaola		●									●																	●				
The Rainbow Fish, Marcus Pfister						●					●																		●			
The Relatives Came, Cynthia Rylant									●		●													●		●			●		●	
The Reptile Room, Lemony Snicket * - Ch. 1		●											●											●			●			●		
The Seashore Book, Charlotte Zolotow								●																								
The Slippery Slope, Lemony Snicket * - Ch. 1	●	●									●	●	●								●						●	●	●			●
The Snowy Day, Ezra Jack Keats																						●				●						
The Tale of Despereaux, Kate DiCamillo * - Ch. 1		●				●						●	●										●			●						

Title																																
The Talking Eggs, Robert D. San Souci									●		●										●								●	●	●	●
The Ticky-Tacky Doll, Cynthia Rylant	●	●				●					●																			●	●	●
The True Story of the Three Little Pigs, Jon Scieszka		●										●											●	●	●				●	●		●
The Underwater Alphabet Book, Jerry Pallotta				●									●														●					
The Very Busy Spider, Eric Carle																						●		●								
The Very Hungry Caterpillar, Eric Carle	●										●													●					●		●	
The Very Quiet Cricket, Eric Carle	●																								●				●			
The Wind Blew, Pat Hutchins																													●			
The World is Your Oyster, Tamara James					●																●											
The Worrywarts, Pamela Duncan Edwards	●																															
Thunder Cake, Patricia Polacco		●							●	●	●															●		●	●		●	
Tigress, Helen Cowcher									●		●				●											●			●	●	●	
Time for Bed, Mem Fox	●																						●	●	●							
Tom, Tomie dePaola		●	●																		●				●						
Tops & Bottoms, Janet Stevens						●																		●		●						
Town Mouse, Country Mouse, Jan Brett										●	●	●														●		●	●	●		
Train Song, Diana Siebert	●																					●	●	●	●			●	●			
Tuesday, David Wiesner									●	●																					●	
Twilight Comes Twice, Ralph Fletcher	●										●										●		●				●					
Two Bad Ants, Chris Van Allsburg										●	●																				●	
Verdi, Janell Cannon									●		●											●							●			
Waiting for Wings, Lois Ehlert											●				●																	
Walk Two Moons, Sharon Creech * - Ch. 1		●																										●	●		●	●
Wanted...Mud Blossom, Betsy Byars * - Ch. 1			●							●											●					●						
We're Going on a Bear Hunt, Michael Rosen																						●		●	●							
What Was I Scared Of?, Dr. Seuss	●																						●	●	●			●	●		●	●
When I Was Young in the Mountains, Cynthia Rylant										●	●													●		●		●			●	●
When the Cows Come Home, by David L. Harrison															●									●	●				●		●	
Where Once There Was a Wood, Denise Fleming	●								●	●														●								
Where the Red Fern Grows, Wilson Rawls * - Ch. 1		●									●										●						●				●	●
Where the Wild Things Are, Maurice Sendak						●					●													●		●			●	●	●	
White Snow, Bright Snow, Alvin Tresselt											●												●	●				●	●			
Zin! Zin! Zin! A Violin, Lloyd Moss											●											●	●	●	●			●	●			

FICTION LITERATURE-MODEL MATRIX

YOUR FICTION LITERATURE-MODEL MATRIX

Title and Author

VOICE
TRANSITIONS: TIME
TRANSITIONS: PLACE
STRONG VERBS
SPECIFICITY
SIMILE
SENTENCE VARIATION
RHYME
REPETITION
PERSONIFICATION
ONOMATOPOEIA
METAPHOR
LETTER FORMATS
HYPERBOLE
UNIVERSAL WORD

ENDING TECHNIQUE
REMIND THE READER
QUESTION
CIRCLE BACK TO THE HOOK
ADVICE TO THE READER

EMBEDDED DEFINITION
DIALOGUE TAGS
DESCRIPTIVE ATTRIBUTES
CLUES FOR INFERENCE

BEGINNING TECHNIQUE
SETTING
QUESTION
ONOMATOPOEIA
INTRO OF MAIN CHARACTER
IDIOM
EXCLAMATION
DIALOGUE

ASIDES TO THE READER
ALLITERATION

About the Non-fiction Literature-model Matrix

In addition to a wealth of creative fiction, your print-rich classroom should also contain many high-quality non-fiction texts. In addition to content-area learning, you can use these books to point out organizational structure, understand main ideas and supporting details, and demonstrate for students the value of engaging text.

The types of skills often found in non-fiction vary from what is found in fiction. Therefore, the skills listed on the matrix differ slightly. As discussed in Chapter Two, age-appropriate magazines contain many well-written non-fiction articles that can be used to model writing-craft skills. Newspaper articles often provide examples of beginning and ending techniques, supporting details, and character and setting descriptions. Keep a file of newspaper and magazine articles to supplement your classroom collection of literature models.

NON-FICTION LITERATURE-MODEL MATRIX

Title and Author		BEGINNING TECHNIQUE						ENDING TECHNIQUE															
	ALLITERATION	DIALOGUE	EXCLAMATION	ONOMATOPOEIA	QUESTION	SETTING	DESCRIPTIVE ATTRIBUTES	EMBEDDED DEFINITION	ADVICE TO THE READER	CIRCLE BACK TO THE HOOK	QUESTION	REMIND THE READER	UNIVERSAL WORD	ONOMATOPOEIA	PERSONIFICATION	RHYME	SENTENCE VARIATION	SIMILE	SPECIFICITY	STRONG VERBS	TRANSITIONS: PLACE	TRANSITIONS: TIME	VOICE
A Picture Book of Davy Crockett, David A. Adler		●																					
A Picture Book of Lewis and Clark, David A. Adler		●				●																	
A Seed is a Promise, Claire Merrill								●											●			●	●
A Strong Right Arm, Michelle Y. Green																	●	●		●		●	●
A Weed is a Flower: The Life of George Washington Carver, Aliki						●											●					●	
An Octopus is Amazing, Patricia Lauber							●	●									●		●				
And Then What Happened, Paul Revere? Jean Fritz						●											●		●			●	
Animal Dads, Sneed B. Collard III								●		●							●		●	●			●
Ant Cities, Arthur Dorros					●				●										●		●		
Antarctica, Helen Cowcher						●	●													●			
Bats, Gail Gibbons	●						●	●											●				
Blizzard!: The Storm That Changed America, Jim Murphy							●													●	●	●	
Bodies from the Ash: Life and Death in Ancient Pompeii, James M. Deem							●	●									●			●	●	●	
Cactus Hotel, Brenda Z. Guiberson						●	●			●				●					●	●			
Check It Out!: The Book About Libraries, Gail Gibbons							●		●										●				
Children of the Wild West, Russell Freedman							●													●			
Digging Up Dinosaurs, Aliki					●																		
Dolphins!, Margaret Davidson					●								●				●			●			
Everglades, Jean Craighead George							●										●	●	●				●
Fireflies in the Night, Judy Hawes																	●						
Flash, Crash, Rumble, and Roll, Franklyn M. Branley						●						●					●			●			
Forensics, Richard Platt																	●			●			●
Fossils Tell of Long Ago, Aliki								●									●						
From Seed to Plant, Gail Gibbons							●										●		●				
Germs Make Me Sick!, Melvin Berger								●															●
Growing Colors, Bruce McMillan							●																
Growing Frogs, Vivian French							●	●															

How Big Were the Dinosaurs?, Bernard Most																			●				●
It's a Good Thing There Are Insects, Allan Fowler							●	●				●							●				
Kites Sail High: A Book About Verbs, Ruth Heller																●				●			
Martin's Big Words: The Life of Dr. Martin Luther King, Jr, Doreen Rappaport						●											●					●	●
Moja Means One: Swahili Counting Book, Muriel Feelings																			●				●
Mojave, Diane Siebert					●		●			●					●					●			
My Five Senses, Aliki			●					●															
My Hands, Aliki			●								●									●			
My Visit to the Aquarium, Aliki												●							●				
Oil Spill, Melvin Berger						●		●											●	●			
Plants That Never Bloom, Ruth Heller							●	●											●				
Puffins Climb, Penguins Rhyme, Bruce McMillan	●																			●			
Quilted Landscape, Yale Strom							●														●	●	●
Rain, Robert Kalan							●										●						
Rain Forest Secrets, Arthur Dorros					●		●	●			●								●		●		●
Recycle!: A Handbook for Kids, Gail Gibbons			●					●									●		●				
Shoes, Shoes, Shoes, Ann Morris							●												●	●			
Sixteen Years in Sixteen Seconds, Paula Yoo																	●		●	●			
Snakes Are Hunters, Patricia Lauber							●			●								●	●	●			
So That's How the Moon Changes Shape!, Allan Fowler												●											
So You Want to Be President?, Judith St. George							●		●				●				●						●
Sunken Treasure, Gail Gibbons		●						●									●						
The Cloud Book, Tomie dePaola												●					●						●
The Great Serum Race: Blazing the Iditarod Trail, Debbie S. Miller																			●	●	●	●	
The Honey Makers, Gail Gibbons						●	●	●		●								●					
The Magic School Bus Inside the Earth, Joanna Cole						●	●	●		●							●		●	●	●		●
The Magic School Bus Inside a Beehive, Joanna Cole		●					●	●		●							●		●	●	●		●
The Milk Makers, Gail Gibbons								●															
The Moon Book, Gail Gibbons	●						●	●															
Through My Eyes, Ruby Bridges									●						●				●			●	
Volcano: The Eruption and Healing of Mount St. Helens, Patricia Lauber							●	●							●		●		●	●		●	
Wackiest White House Pets, Kathryn Gibbs Davis													●				●	●	●	●		●	

NON-FICTION LITERATURE-MODEL MATRIX

BEGINNING TECHNIQUE / ENDING TECHNIQUE

Title and Author	ALLITERATION	DIALOGUE	EXCLAMATION	ONOMATOPOEIA	QUESTION	SETTING	DESCRIPTIVE ATTRIBUTES	EMBEDDED DEFINITION	ADVICE TO THE READER	CIRCLE BACK TO THE HOOK	QUESTION	REMIND THE READER	UNIVERSAL WORD	ONOMATOPOEIA	PERSONIFICATION	RHYME	SENTENCE VARIATION	SIMILE	SPECIFICITY	STRONG VERBS	TRANSITIONS: PLACE	TRANSITIONS: TIME	VOICE
What Happened to the Dinosaurs?, Franklyn Branley										●								●	●				
What Happens to a Hamburger?, Paul Showers								●											●	●			●
When is a Planet Not a Planet?: The Story of Pluto, Elaine Scott							●	●									●		●			●	
Who Eats What? Food Chains and Food Webs, Patricia Lauber																				●		●	●
Zipping, Zapping, Zooming Bats, Ann Earle	●							●											●	●			

YOUR NON-FICTION LITERATURE-MODEL MATRIX

BEGINNING TECHNIQUE / ENDING TECHNIQUE

Title and Author	ALLITERATION	DIALOGUE	EXCLAMATION	ONOMATOPOEIA	QUESTION	SETTING	DESCRIPTIVE ATTRIBUTES	EMBEDDED DEFINITION	ADVICE TO THE READER	CIRCLE BACK TO THE HOOK	QUESTION	REMIND THE READER	UNIVERSAL WORD	ONOMATOPOEIA	PERSONIFICATION	RHYME	SENTENCE VARIATION	SIMILE	SPECIFICITY	STRONG VERBS	TRANSITIONS: PLACE	TRANSITIONS: TIME	VOICE

About the Poetry Literature-model Matrix

Poetry is often brief, making writing-craft Target Skills easy to identify. Short poems can be displayed on chart paper or broadcast via LCD projector so that all students can view and hear the example of writing craft. As with non-fiction, you will find that the skills listed in the poetry matrix differ slightly from the fiction matrix.

Because practice pieces should be brief and targeted, assigning poetry that demonstrates particular writing-craft Target Skills is a valuable workshop activity. Students can apply skills within a brief context, giving them a sense of completeness and wholeness that makes them more likely to go back and revise. Therefore, use poetry to model both skills and format.

POETRY LITERATURE-MODEL MATRIX

Title and Author		Beginning Technique						Ending Technique														
	Alliteration	Dialogue	Exclamation	Question	Clues for Inference	Descriptive Attributes	Dialogue Tags	Circle Back to the Hook	Feeling Statement	Universal Word	Hyperbole	Metaphor	Onomatopoeia	Personification	Repetition	Rhyme	Simile	Specificity	Strong Verbs	Transitions: Place	Transitions: Time	Voice
"8 A.M. Shadows" - Patricia Hubbell											●				●	●			●			
"A Pizza the Size of the Sun" - Jack Prelutsky											●				●	●		●				
"A True Story" - Brod Bagert			●													●			●			
"Alexander's Breakfast" - Brod Bagert						●										●		●				
"April Rain Song" - Langston Hughes									●					●	●				●			
"Bad Cold" - Shel Silverstein											●		●			●						●
"Be Glad Your Nose is on Your Face" - Jack Prelutsky																●			●			●
"Big Little Boy" - Eve Merriam		●					●				●						●					
"Bugs! Bugs!" - Jack Prelutsky			●			●				●												
"Cats" - Eleanor Farjeon								●								●				●		
"Cereal" - Shel Silverstein						●							●					●				●
"City" - Langston Hughes														●	●	●					●	
"Clickbeetle" - Mary Ann Hoberman	●							●					●		●	●						
"Clouds" - Christina Rossetti												●			●	●						
"Crickets" - Valerie Worth						●								●					●			
"Dandelion" - Hilda Conkling				●		●						●										
"Dauntless Dimble" - Jack Prelutsky	●				●											●			●			
"Diving Board" - Shel Silverstein					●										●	●						●
"Don't Tell Me That I Talk Too Much!" - Arnold Spilka			●													●						●
"Dreams" - Langston Hughes												●			●	●						
"Easter" - Joyce Kilmer						●								●		●	●					
"Eat-it-All Elaine" - Kay Starbird					●											●		●		●	●	
"Every Time I Climb a Tree" - David McCord										●					●	●						
"Eyeballs for Sale" - Jack Prelutsky			●					●								●						
"Fall Feelings" - Margriet Ruurs	●			●		●								●		●			●			
"Feather or Fur" - John Becker	●							●							●	●						
"Feelings About Words" - Mary O'Neill						●							●	●		●	●		●			

"Flowers are a Silly Bunch" - Arnold Spilka						●			●					●		●						
"Fog" - Carl Sandburg														●								
"Galoshes" - Rhoda Bacmeister	●												●			●						
"Happy Birthday, Dear Dragon" - Jack Prelutsky							●									●		●	●			
"Here Comes the Band" - William Cole	●												●			●						
"Houses" - Mary Britton Miller	●					●										●		●				
"Hug O' War" - Shel Silverstein										●						●			●			
"I Am Cherry Alive" - Delmore Schwartz		●					●								●	●						
"I Am Running in a Circle" - Jack Prelutsky															●	●						
"I Heard a Bird Sing" - Oliver Herford					●			●							●	●					●	
"I'm Alone in the Evening" - Michael Rosen													●			●			●		●	
"I'm Bold, I'm Brave" - Jack Prelutsky					●											●						
"In the Motel" - X. J. Kennedy			●		●				●							●			●			
"Invention" - Shel Silverstein			●																			●
"Knoxville, Tennessee" - Nikki Giovanni																		●				
"Leave Me Alone" - Felice Holman			●													●						●
"Llook!" - Jack Prelutsky	●																					
"maggie and milly and molly and may" - E.E. Cummings	●															●	●		●			
"Mice" - Rose Fyleman						●			●							●						
"Moose Meadow" - Margriet Ruurs	●																	●		●		
"Mountain Brook" - Elizabeth Coatsworth						●										●	●					
"Mud" - Polly Chase Boyden			●			●			●							●						
"Night" - Mary Ann Hoberman														●					●			●
"Night Creature" - Lilian Moore						●			●					●					●			
"No Thank You" - Shel Silverstein	●					●									●	●						
"Oh Please Take Me Fishing" - Jack Prelutsky		●					●									●			●			
"On Our Way" - Eve Merriam				●												●	●		●			
"On the Ning Nang Nong" - Spike Milligan	●												●		●	●						
"Our Tree" - Marchette Chute									●							●					●	
"Paper II" - Carl Sandburg	●					●	●							●								
"Pie Problem" - Shel Silverstein											●		●			●						

POETRY LITERATURE-MODEL MATRIX		BEGINNING TECHNIQUE						ENDING TECHNIQUE														
Title and Author	ALLITERATION	DIALOGUE	EXCLAMATION	QUESTION	CLUES FOR INFERENCE	DESCRIPTIVE ATTRIBUTES	DIALOGUE TAGS	CIRCLE BACK TO THE HOOK	FEELING STATEMENT	UNIVERSAL WORD	HYPERBOLE	METAPHOR	ONOMATOPOEIA	PERSONIFICATION	REPETITION	RHYME	SIMILE	SPECIFICITY	STRONG VERBS	TRANSITIONS: PLACE	TRANSITIONS: TIME	VOICE
"Poetry" - Eleanor Farjeon				●				●								●						
"Rhyme" - Elizabeth Coatsworth						●									●	●						
"Sick" - Shel Silverstein						●										●						●
"Silver" - Walter de la Mare														●		●			●			
"Smells" - Kathryn Worth						●										●						
"Sneaky Sue" - Jack Prelutsky																●			●	●		
"Soap" - Martin Gardner			●													●						●
"Some One" - Walter de la Mare										●						●			●			
"Some People" - Rachel Field					●											●	●					
"Spring" - Karla Kuskin					●											●			●			
"Spring Is" - Bobbi Katz														●			●		●			
"Stagefright" - Margriet Ruurs																	●		●			
"Sulk" - Felice Holman																●			●			
"Sunrise" - Frank Asch														●		●						
"Swing, Swing" - William Allingham					●						●				●	●						
"The Bear, The Fire, and The Snow" - Shel Silverstein						●		●						●		●			●			
"The Famous Purple Poka Bear" - Brod Bagert						●				●												
"The Fummawummalummazumms" - Jack Prelutsky	●														●	●			●			
"The Lesser Lynx" - E.V. Rieu	●															●						
"The Moon's the North Wind's Cookie" - Vachel Lindsay												●				●						
"The Night is a Big Black Cat" - G. Orr Clark												●				●						
"The Toad" - Robert S. Oliver																●					●	
"They're Calling" - Felice Holman		●			●		●															
"They've All Gone South" - Mary Britton Miller						●										●		●				
"Train Song" - Diane Siebert	●												●			●		●				
"Valentine" - Shel Silverstein																●		●				●
"Virtual Maniac" - Margriet Ruurs			●				●						●			●						

"Waking" - Lilian Moore									●									●				
"What is Pink?" - Christina Rossetti				●		●										●						
"What is Red?" - Mary O'Neill						●						●				●			●			
"What's That?" - Florence Parry Heide				●		●										●						
"Who Has Seen the Wind" - Christina Rossetti				●											●	●						
"Who's In" - Elizabeth Fleming		●								●					●	●						
"Winter Moon" - Langston Hughes			●			●									●	●						
"Windy Nights" - Robert Louis Stevenson						●										●			●		●	

YOUR POETRY LITERATURE-MODEL MATRIX

	Beginning Technique							Ending Technique														
Title and Author	Alliteration	Dialogue	Exclamation	Question	Clues for Inference	Descriptive Attributes	Dialogue Tags	Circle Back to the Hook	Feeling Statement	Universal Word	Hyperbole	Metaphor	Onomatopoeia	Personification	Repetition	Rhyme	Simile	Specificity	Strong Verbs	Transitions: Place	Transitions: Time	Voice

About the Spanish Literature-model Matrix

In our increasingly diverse society, we recognize the need to support teachers of English-language learners. Many children's literature titles have been translated into Spanish and are available for classroom use. For this reason, we have included a matrix devoted to Spanish translations available for many of the titles listed on the fiction and non-fiction matrices.

SPANISH LITERATURE-MODEL MATRIX

SPANISH LITERATURE-MODEL MATRIX

Title and Author	Alliteration	Asides to the Reader	Dialogue	Exclamation	Intro of Main Character	Onomatopoeia	Question	Setting	Clues for Inference	Descriptive Attributes	Dialogue Tags	Embedded Definition	Advice to the Reader	Circle Back to the Hook	Question	Remind the Reader	Universal Word	Hyperbole	Letter Formats	Metaphor	Onomatopoeia	Personification	Repetition	Rhyme	Sentence Variation	Simile	Specificity	Strong Verbs	Transitions: Place	Transitions: Time	Voice
			Beginning Technique										Ending Technique																		
Abran Paso a Los Patitos, Robert McCloskey											●																●				
Alexander y el Día Terrible, Horrible, Espantoso, Horroroso, Judith Viorst										●															●						●
Amos y Boris, William Steig																							●		●		●				
Buenas Noches, Luna, Margaret Wise Brown								●										●					●	●							
Calabaza, Calabaza, Jeanne Titherington										●																					
Ciudades de Hormigas, Arthur Dorros							●						●														●		●		
Clic, Clac, Muu: Vacas Escritoras, Doreen Cronin	●																		●		●										
Colors! ¡Colores!, Jorge Lujan										●										●		●	●			●		●			
Corduroy, Don Freeman					●				●																				●	●	
Crisantemo, Kevin Henkes										●	●																●				
Crispín: La Cruz de Plomo, Avi * - Cap. 1									●		●											●			●		●	●	●	●	
Cuaquito, Lauren Thompson	●																				●										
Despereaux, Kate DiCamillo		●			●						●	●										●			●						
Detective LaRue: Cartas de la Investigación, Mark Teague										●									●						●						●
Donde Viven los Monstruos, Maurice Sendak					●					●															●			●	●	●	
El Ascensor Ingenioso, Lemony Snicket * - Cap. 1		●							●		●	●															●				●
El Arbol Generoso, Shel Silverstein					●																	●	●							●	
¿El Canguro Tiene Mamá?, Eric Carle				●										●									●	●							
El Expreso Polar, Chris Van Allsburg									●	●															●			●			
El Gato En el Sombrero, Dr. Seuss															●								●	●							
El Hacha, Gary Paulsen * - Cap. 10									●	●															●			●			
El Hueso Prodigioso, William Steig																						●						●			
El Libro de Las Nubes, Tomie dePaola										●						●									●						
El Lorax, Dr. Seuss								●									●						●						●	●	●
El Pez Arco Iris, Marcus Pfister					●					●																		●			
El Poni de Barro, Caron Lee Cohen					●				●																				●	●	

Title																															
Entre Dos Lunas, Sharon Creech * - Cap.1	●	●		●	●																									●	
Esperanza Renace, Pam Muñoz Ryan * - Cap. 1				●			●																●						●		
Froggy Se Viste, Jonathan London											●										●										
Gracias a Winn-Dixie, Kate DiCamillo					●		●														●	●	●				●				
Irene, la valiente, William Steig	●		●	●			●			●											●	●									
James y el Melocotón Gigante, Roald Dahl * - Cap. 1	●			●	●																●	●								●	
Jumanji, Chris Van Allsburg				●																	●	●							●		
La Araña Muy Ocupada, Eric Carle				●					●		●																				
La Habitación de los Reptiles, Lemony Snicket * - Cap. 1		●		●		●			●											●										●	
La Mariquita Malhumorada, Eric Carle		●	●	●	●													●				●		●							
La Oruga Muy Hambrienta, Eric Carle		●		●					●													●			●						●
La Pequeña Locomotora Que Sí Pudo, Watty Piper					●				●	●	●															●					
La Señorita Runfio, Barbara Cooney		●		●																		●					●				
La Telaraña de Carlota, E.B. White * - Cap. 1				●																	●	●			●				●		
La Telaraña de Carlota, E.B. White * - Cap. 3	●		●	●	●		●												●		●	●	●	●							
La Telaraña de Carlota, E.B. White * - Cap. 4		●		●			●		●													●	●								
¡La Verdadera Historia de los Tres Cerditos!, Jon Scieszka	●		●	●				●	●	●											●									●	
Las Rimas de Mamá Oca, CD Hullinger								●	●																						●
Los Verdaderas Aventuras de Hank, el Perro Vaquero, John R. Erickson *	●						●																				●				
Me Llamo Bud, No Buddy, Christopher Paul Curtis * - Cap. 9	●			●	●		●					●									●	●									
Mike Mulligan y su Máquina Maravillosa, Virginia Burton									●	●												●					●				
Mis Cinco Sentidos, Aliki									●											●								●			
Mis Manos, Aliki				●													●											●			
Nadarín, Leo Lionni		●	●	●								●										●									
Niño Cuervo, Taro Yashima										●	●									●											
Oso Pardo, Oso Pardo, ¿Qué Ves Ahí?, Bill Martin								●	●													●									
Pecos Bill, Steven Kellogg	●			●										●																	
Puente hasta Terabithia, Katherine Paterson * - Cap. 1				●		●					●															●					
Pinta Ratones, Ellen Stoll Walsh																						●									
El Pollo de los Domingos, Patricia Polacco					●	●	●		●												●										
Querida Sra. LaRue: Cartas desde la Academia Canina, Mark Teague	●						●					●	●									●									
Querido Salvatierra, Simon James		●		●									●									●									

SPANISH LITERATURE-MODEL MATRIX

SPANISH LITERATURE-MODEL MATRIX

Technique		*Querido Señor Henshaw*, Beverly Cleary	*Ramona la Chinche*, Beverly Cleary	*Sarah, Sencillá y Alta*, Patricia MacLachlan * - Cap. 1	*Se Venden Gorras*, Esphyr Slobodkina	*Si le das un Panecillo a un Alce*, Laura Numeroff	*Si le das una Galletita a un Ratón*, Laura Numeroff	*Si le das un Panqueque a una Cerdita*, Laura Numeroff	*Silvestre y la Piedrecita Magica*, William Steig	*Stelaluna*, Janell Cannon	*Strega Nona*, Tomie dePaola	*Stuart Little*, E.B. White	*¿Tu Mamá es una Llama?*, Deborah Guarino	*Un Dia de Nieve*, Ezra Jack Keets	*Un Mal Principio*, Lemony Snicket * - Cap. 1	*Vamos a Cazar un Oso*, Michael Rosen	*Verdi*, Janell Cannon
	VOICE	●		●		●	●	●							●		
	TRANSITIONS: TIME								●		●						
	TRANSITIONS: PLACE								●	●	●						
	STRONG VERBS		●	●						●	●	●			●		●
	SPECIFICITY										●	●					
	SIMILE			●						●							
	SENTENCE VARIATION		●	●						●		●	●	●	●		
	RHYME										●		●			●	
	REPETITION										●		●			●	
	PERSONIFICATION			●						●							
	ONOMATOPOEIA				●									●		●	●
	METAPHOR																
	LETTER FORMATS	●															
	HYPERBOLE																
	UNIVERSAL WORD								●								
ENDING TECHNIQUE	REMIND THE READER																
ENDING TECHNIQUE	QUESTION																
ENDING TECHNIQUE	CIRCLE BACK TO THE HOOK					●	●	●						●			
ENDING TECHNIQUE	ADVICE TO THE READER																
	EMBEDDED DEFINITION														●		
	DIALOGUE TAGS		●	●						●					●		
	DESCRIPTIVE ATTRIBUTES		●	●	●					●	●	●			●		●
	CLUES FOR INFERENCE	●											●		●		
	SETTING									●							●
BEGINNING TECHNIQUE	QUESTION												●				
BEGINNING TECHNIQUE	ONOMATOPOEIA																
BEGINNING TECHNIQUE	INTRO OF MAIN CHARACTER								●		●	●					
BEGINNING TECHNIQUE	EXCLAMATION																
BEGINNING TECHNIQUE	DIALOGUE		●	●									●				
	ASIDES TO THE READER														●		
	ALLITERATION																

YOUR SPANISH LITERATURE-MODEL MATRIX

Title and Author

- VOICE
- TRANSITIONS: TIME
- TRANSITIONS: PLACE
- STRONG VERBS
- SPECIFICITY
- SIMILE
- SENTENCE VARIATION
- RHYME
- REPETITION
- PERSONIFICATION
- ONOMATOPOEIA
- METAPHOR
- LETTER FORMATS
- HYPERBOLE
- UNIVERSAL WORD

ENDING TECHNIQUE

- REMIND THE READER
- QUESTION
- CIRCLE BACK TO THE HOOK
- ADVICE TO THE READER
- EMBEDDED DEFINITION
- DIALOGUE TAGS
- DESCRIPTIVE ATTRIBUTES
- CLUES FOR INFERENCE
- SETTING

BEGINNING TECHNIQUE

- QUESTION
- ONOMATOPOEIA
- INTRO OF MAIN CHARACTER
- EXCLAMATION
- DIALOGUE
- ASIDES TO THE READER
- ALLITERATION

Bibliography

Professional Books:

Barrett, Judi. *Animals Should Definitely Not Wear Clothing.* New York: Aladdin, 2006.

Brown, Laurie Krasny. *How to Be a Friend: A Guide to Making Friends and Keeping Them.* 1998. Reprint, New York: Little, Brown Young Readers, 2001.

Calkins, Lucy. *The Art of Teaching Writing.* New ed. Chicago: Heinemann, 1994.

Carlson, Nancy. *How to Lose All Your Friends.* 1994. Reprint, New York City: Puffin, 1997.

Cohen, Caron Lee. *The Mud Pony: A Traditional Skidi Pawnee Tale.* New York: Scholastic, 1988.

Cowell, Cressida. *How to Train Your Dragon Book 1.* New York: Little, Brown Books for Young Readers, 2010.

Dahlie, Elizabeth. *Bernelly & Harriet: The Country Mouse and the City Mouse.* 1st ed. Boston: Little, Brown, 2002.

Dakos, Kalli. *The Greatest Magic: Poems for Teachers.* New York: Scholastic, 2000.

dePaola, Tomie. *The Popcorn Book.* New York: Holiday House, 1984.

Fleming, Denise. *Where Once There Was a Wood.* New York: Henry Holt & Company, 2000.

Freeman, Marcia S. *Building a Writing Community: A Practical Guide.* Gainesville: Maupin House Publishing, 1995.

Freeman, Marcia S. *Listen to This: Developing an Ear for Expository.* Gainesville: Maupin House Publishing, 1997.

Freeman, Marcia S., Luana K. Mitten, and Rachel M. Chappell. *Models for Teaching Writing-Craft Target Skills.* Gainesville: Maupin House Publishing, 2005.

George, Jean Craighead. *Everglades.* New York: HarperCollins Publishers, 1997.

George, Judith St. *So You Want to be President? Revised and Updated Edition.* New York: Philomel, 2004.

Gibbons, Gail. *From Seed to Plant.* New York: Holiday House, 1993.

Graham, S., and M. A. Herbert. *Writing to Read: Evidence for How Writing Can Improve Reading. A Carnegie Corporation Time to Act Report*. Washington, DC: Alliance for Excellent Education, 2010.

Graves, Donald H. *A Fresh Look at Writing.* Chicago: Heinemann, 1994.

Graves, Donald H. *A Sea of Faces: The Importance of Knowing Your Students.* Chicago: Heinemann, 2006.

Gregorian, Vartan. Foreword to *Writing to Read: Evidence for How Writing Can Improve Reading. A Carnegie Corporation Time to Act Report*, by S. Graham, and M.A. Hebert. Washington, DC: Alliance for Excellent Education, 2010.

Heard, Georgia, ed. *Falling Down the Page: A Book of List Poems.* New Milford: Roaring Brook Press, 2009.

Holt, Dan. "What Coaching Football Taught Me about Teaching Writing." *The Voice* 4, no. 3, 1999. (Web accessed 14 July 2010).

Koehler, Susan. *Purposeful Writing Assessment: Using Multiple-Choice Practice to Inform Writing Instruction.* Gainesville: Maupin House Publishing, 2008.

Marzano, Robert J. *What Works in Schools: Translating Research into Action.* Alexandria, VA: Association for Supervision and Curriculum Development, 2003.

McCloskey, Robert. *Blueberries for Sal.* New York: Viking Press, 1976.

Provost, Gary. *100 Ways to Improve Your Writing: Proven Professional Techniques for Writing With Style and Power.* New York: Mentor Books, 1985.

Remkiewicz, Frank. "Illustrating a Book is Kind of Like This," in *Listen to This: Developing an Ear for Expository*, by Marcia S. Freeman, 65. Gainesville: Maupin House Publishing, 2003.

Scholes, Robert. *The Rise and Fall of English: Reconstructing English as a Discipline.* New Haven: Yale University Press, 1999.

Shanahan, T. "Reading-writing Relationships, Thematic Units, Inquiry Learning . . . In Pursuit of Effective Integrated Literacy Instruction." *The Reading Teacher* 51.1 (1997): 12-19.

Van Allsburg, Chis. *Just a Dream.* New York: Scholastic, 1992.

Writing Study Group of the NCTE Executive Committee, The. "NCTE Beliefs about the Teaching of Writing" 2004. *National Council of Teachers of English - Guideline*. (Web accessed 14 July 2010).

Zinsser, William, ed. *Inventing the Truth: The Art and Craft of Memoir.* Boston: Houghton Mifflin Co., 1987.

Poetry Collections*:

Bagert, Brod. *Let Me Be . . . The Boss: Poems for Kids to Perform.* Honesdale: Boyds Mills Press, 1995.

Baxter, Nicola, ed. *The Children's Classic Poetry Collection.* New York: Smithmark Publishers, 1996.

Prelutsky, Jack. *A Pizza the Size of the Sun.* New York: Greenwillow Books, 1996.

Prelutsky, Jack, ed. *The Random House Book of Poetry for Children: A Treasury of 572 Poems for Today's Child.* New York: Random House, 1983.

Regniers, Beatrice Schenk de, and others, eds. *Sing a Song of Popcorn: Every Child's Book of Poems.* New York: Scholastic Press, 1988.

Ruurs, Margriet. *Virtual Maniac: Silly and Serious Poems for Kids.* Gainesville: Maupin House Publishing, 2000.

Silverstein, Shel. *Where the Sidewalk Ends.* New York: Harper & Row, 1974.

Silverstein, Shel. *Falling Up.* New York: HarperCollins Publisher, 1996.

*All of the poems listed in the "Poetry Literature-model Matrix" can be found in these books.

Notes

Notes

Notes

Notes